Aadhaar

Published by
ACADEMIC FOUNDATION
in association with

HEINRICH BÖLL STIFTUNG
INDIA

ABOUT THE AUTHORS:

Govind Kelkar is a senior advisor to Landesa, India. She formerly headed Women's Economic Empowerment Unit at UN Women, South Asia Office, New Delhi. She has authored and co-authored 12 books, 48 research papers, and has been a founder-editor of *Gender, Technology and Development Journal*.

Dev Nathan is professor at the Institute for Human Development, Delhi and Visiting Research Fellow at Duke University, USA. He is also an editor of the series: *Development Trajectories in Global Value Chains*.

E. Revathi is Professor at the Centre for Economic and Social Studies (CESS), Hyderabad, Telangana State. Her areas of research are: development studies, agriculture, gender studies and regional inequalities, with attention to land and women's empowerment.

Swati Sain Gupta is an international development professional who has worked in and led several development organisations in Latin America, Europe and India. Currently she coordinates PLATFORMA, the network of European local and regional governments.

Aadhaar

Gender, Identity and Development

GOVIND KELKAR
DEV NATHAN
E. REVATHI
SWATI SAIN GUPTA

ACADEMIC FOUNDATION
NEW DELHI

www.academicfoundation.com

First published in 2014
by

ACADEMIC FOUNDATION
4772-73 / 23 Bharat Ram Road, (23 Ansari Road),
Darya Ganj, New Delhi - 110 002 (India).
Phones : 23245001 / 02 / 03 / 04.
Fax : +91-11-23245005.
E-mail : books@academicfoundation.com
www.academicfoundation.com

in association with
The Heinrich Böll Stiftung/Foundation (HBF).

Cataloging in Publication Data--DK
Courtesy: D.K. Agencies (P) Ltd. <docinfo@dkagencies.com>

Aadhaar: gender, identity and development / Govind Kelkar ... [et al.].
p. cm.
Includes bibliographical references (p.).
ISBN 9789332701687

1. Biometric identification cards--India. 2. Gender identity--India. 3. Women--Services for--India. 4. Women in development--India. 5. Human services--India. I. Kelkar, Govind, 1939-

DDC 323.4483 23

Typeset by Italics India, New Delhi.

Printed and bound by The Book Mint, New Delhi.
www.thebookmint.in

CONTENTS

List of Abbreviations

ADB.......................Asian Development Bank
AEPS.......................Aadhaar Enabled Payment System
APDPIP.................Andhra Pradesh District Poverty Initiatives Project
APB.......................Aadhaar Payments Bridge
APRPRP.................Andhra Pradesh Rural Poverty Reduction Project
AWWs...................Anganwadi Workers
BCs.......................Business Correspondents
BPL.......................Below Poverty Line
CBA.......................Cost Benefit Analysis
CSP.......................Community Service Provider
DBT.......................Direct Benefits Transfer
DC.......................District Coordinator
DSE.......................District Superintendents of Education
DWCRA.................Development of Women and Children in Rural Areas
EID.......................Enrolment Identity
FGD.......................Focus Group Discussion
FPS.......................Fair Price Shop
GDP.......................Gross Domestic Product
GEMI.....................Gender Empowerment Measure Index
GoI.......................Government of India
GoJH.....................Government of Jharkhand
GPS.......................Global Positioning System
HAS.......................Hindu Succession Act
HYV.......................High Yielding Varieties
IAY.......................Indira Awas Yojana
ICDS.....................Integrated Child Development Scheme

ICRW......................International Center for Research on Women
ID Card..................Identity Card
IRR.........................Internal Rate of Return
IKP.........................Indira Kranthi Patham
IMF.........................International Monetary Fund
KYC........................Know Your Customer
JSY.........................Janani Suraksha Yojana
LPG.........................Liquefied Petroleum Gas
MC..........................Mandal Coordinator
MGNREGA............Mahatma Gandhi National Rural Employment Guarantee Act
MGNREGS............Mahatma Gandhi National Rural Employment Guarantee Act Scheme
MoU.......................Memorandum of Understanding
NGO.......................Non-governmental Organisation
NIPFP....................National Institute of Public Finance and Policy
NTFP.....................Non-Timber Forest Products
PDS........................Public Distribution System
POS........................Point-of-Sale
PRAN.....................Permanent Retirement Account Number
SAPAP...................South Asia Poverty Alleviation Programme
SERP......................Society for Elimination of Rural Poverty
SHG.......................Self-Help Group
SIDA......................Swedish International Development Agency
SSP........................Social Security Payment
TSP........................Technical Service Provider
UID........................Unique Identification
UIDAI....................Unique Identification Authority of India
VRA.......................Village Revenue Assistant

Preface

Aadhaar, the biometry-based identification system operated by the Unique Identification Authority of India (UIDAI), is designed to provide every person living in India with an individual ID which can be used for a variety of purposes. Aadhaar has been rapidly expanding in the last few years, and by mid-2014, it covered about half of the country's population. In July 2014, the new government under Prime Minister Narendra Modi affirmed its intention to move forward with the Aadhaar scheme, strengthen its legal status and employ it for the delivery of various social benefits. This decision ended a period of election-related uncertainty about the future of the scheme.

With this, it is clear that Aadhaar is going to become an important instrument to deliver government services in India. Aadhaar is also likely to make it easier for Indians—particularly those of the disadvantaged background—to access services by private providers which require the presentation of personal ID documents, such as opening a bank account or acquiring a mobile phone SIM card.

This book looks at the gender dimension of Aadhaar, studying the (current and potential) impact of the scheme especially on women and on gender relationships within the household. Very little (if any) attention has been given to this question up to now.

Instead, the major debate around Aadhaar has always been whether the scheme will accomplish its declared objective of achieving greater efficiency in the provision of services, or whether it may lead to exclusion from services, or even invite misuse through violations of privacy. This book, while taking an overall positive view on the potentials of Aadhaar, does not address these latter questions in any greater detail. Instead, simply put, it asks the question: What's in for women?

The book analyses the way in which the Aadhaar unique identification scheme provides specific opportunities especially for women, foremost by allowing women to obtain a documentation of identity that is both individual, i.e. independent from the (stereo) typical women's role as wife or daughter within a male-dominated family, and portable, i.e. independent from a particular locality where the document has been issued, and for which it is valid. From this perspective, Aadhaar is a personal identification scheme of choice for women in a society with a rapidly increasing social and geographical mobility.

As it becomes clear in the course of this book, Aadhaar indeed has much potential for strengthening the position of women *vis-à-vis* public institutions and also with regard to their position within the household or family. Of course, much depends on its concrete implementation; Aadhaar does not provide any 'technological quick-fix' for gender equality. However, this books argues that concrete potentials of Aadhaar for gender equality and increased autonomy of women can be identified and should be made practical.

It is high time to implement Aadhaar and the services attached to it in a gender-aware manner, and this book intends to help everybody involved with Aadhaar and the services linked to it—planners, civil servants, political representatives as well as interested members of the general public—to do so.

Axel Harneit-Sievers
Director
Heinrich Böll Foundation, India Office

Acknowledgements

The subject of women's independent identity has, for a long time, been part of feminist discussions. We began research on it while Aadhaar, India's biometric identification system, was being introduced. With limited writings on the subject it was a challenging experience, both conceptually and empirically.

We are indebted to Axel Harneit-Seivers, Director, India Office of the Heinrich Boll Foundation (HBF) for his wisdom in supporting the conduct of this study. He also discussed the framework of the study. It was a joy to work with Shalini Yog, Programme Officer of HBF, who also supplied us many news clippings and resources related to the project. We wish to thank her for her unstinted support, and patience through all the delays that such a study almost inevitably involves.

Dr P.V. Ramesh, at that time Principal Secretary, Ministry of Finance of the then Government of Andhra Pradesh, and also in-charge of Aadhaar implementation in the state, took time off from his busy schedule to share with us his vision and challenges in implementing Aadhaar. We wish to thank him in particular for the wealth of knowledge and commitment to social change which he shared with us during the state level workshop.

Dr D.N. Reddy's professional inputs helped us complete the study in the districts of Andhra Pradesh. Samar Bosu-Mullick, as a scholar and activist in Jharkhand, helped organise meetings of village women and men, as well as meeting with state-level officials. We thank the numerous officials who shared their information in the two states. Naidu and Anil in Andhra Pradesh and Ambar in Jharkhand organised the village meetings. We owe a special thanks to them for organising the meetings in remote villages.

We are grateful to the village women and men who participated in the meetings in the two states.

At the Academic Foundation, our thanks to Sanu Kapila, Sona Kapila, and Uma Kapila for all their support to this publication and their, now customary, good production.

In the end our thanks to the Heinrich Boll Foundation (HBF), a Green Think Tank and policy network, which works with governments and civil society actors, focusing on gender equity, sustainable development, democracy and human rights, for supporting this study.

1

Introduction

Background

In 2006, the Government of India promoted Aadhaar, a biometric identification system, which has now reached 650 million people. The aim of the scheme was to establish a biometric registry to provide a unique identity to all individuals, women and men, in the country. It was expected that this biometric identity would help poor women and men establish their identities so as to access various benefits provided by the government. In conjunction with frugally engineered mini-ATMs (automated teller machines), it was expected to promote financial inclusion.

Would Aadhaar help poor women establish their identity and, through that, secure their entitlements due in various schemes of the government? Would, for instance, widows be able to get their pensions directly in their own hands, rather than have to depend on some male member of the family to get it for them? Would such direct access to benefits help poor women get more control over their entitlements, as against the case of indirect access through male members? Would Aadhaar help women secure dignity and autonomy? In a broad sense, what is the role of identity in development?

These were some of the questions that motivated this study. Besides using secondary material, the study also relied on primary data collected in two districts each of Andhra Pradesh and Jharkhand.

In the rest of this Introduction, the nature and process of the Aadhaar biometric identification system have been outlined. In the chapters that follow, we explore the extent and nature of changes in women's and men's everyday lives, largely as a result of the introduction of Aadhaar Identity. Considering the most local relationship first, the chapters are organised somewhat approximately in terms of research areas where gender relations are differentially constituted, both affecting and reflecting common expectation about acceptable ways of being women or men. We have tried to weave together something about the identity of being a woman or a man and as a material subject for analysis against the background of access to public services. The first three chapters deal with the evolution of Aadhaar policy in addressing the individual need for identification. This is followed by concerns for women's autonomous identity and empowerment. Chapters 4 and 5 discuss the implementation of Aadhaar in two states of India: Andhra Pradesh in the southern part of the country and Jharkhand, a northern state inhabited by indigenous people. These states were selected in view of their initial success in the implementation of Aadhaar technology. The questions of financial inclusion with the help of Aadhaar technology and efficiency with the provision of public services are discussed in chapters 7 and 8. Chapter 9 deals with the nexus of identity, equality and empowerment. The concluding chapter makes a case for needed policy change for enhancing women's capabilities with identity and technology.

What is Aadhaar?

Aadhaar is a 12-digit identity number issued to every individual resident of India. It is based on an individual's name, and other limited demographic and biometric information such as photograph, 10 fingerprints and iris that are unique to an individual. This 12-digit number can be used as a basis to authenticate the identity of the Aadhaar holder in establishing her/his identity or claims to various government services, guaranteed rural employment and access to financial institutions.

The Aadhaar numbers are stored in a centralised database in Central ID Repository, under the management authority of UIDAI (Unique Identification Authority of India), which also provides the authentication services. Reportedly, UIDAI has a robust technology to eliminate duplicate and fake identities in government and private databases.

Aadhaar has a logo of the yellow sun with fingerprints embedded in its centre. The fingerprint incased within the sun symbolises a promise that shines on all equally. Outlining the core value of building an inclusive nation and leveraging Aadhaar to serve all women and men 'effectively, efficiently, and equitably', the Government of India decided to issue unique identification numbers (later came to be called Aadhaar) to all residents in 2007-08. (*https://portal.uidai.gov.in/uidwebportal/dashboard.do*; accessed on 18 June 2014.)

It is not mandatory to any resident of the country to have Aadhaar. However, the government regulations about linking Aadhaar with various public benefits and government services result in making Aadhaar mandatory in practice. The National Identification Authority of India Bill, 2010 (Bill No. LXXV of 2010) was introduced in the Rajya Sabha; the Bill is pending its review and decision of the Parliament.

It is to be noted that Aadhaar is not an entitlement to any public or private service; it acts as a basis of an individual's identity in any part of the country. Aadhaar is a foundational identity with portability of an individual resident's right to identity throughout the country, and therein lays its difference with other identity cards in India: PAN Card, Ration Card, Passport, Driving License, Voter Identity Card and so on.

Two characteristic features of Aadhaar that have been widely talked about are its foundational identity and the related portability of rights. An individual can enrol for Aadhaar anywhere in the country. Unlike in the case of Aadhaar, there is no other identity card in the country that provides a unique identifier to residents and freedom from fake or fraud identities of all kinds. More importantly, a person can have her/his Aadhaar Identity authenticated anywhere and thus be able to access the Aadhaar-linked services from anywhere in the country. However, for this to happen, many significant changes in the service delivery mechanisms need to be made.

The Aadhaar scheme was launched with the aim of establishing a biometric registry of unique identity for all individual women and men throughout the country. The Aadhaar identity was intended to create the opportunity for strengthening efficiency in administration of public programmes and services, financial inclusion and portability of rights to access public services. For example, the Aadhaar number could help rural women or men establish their identity with the banks. As a result, the bank would be able to scale up its branchless banking deployment in rural areas and reach out to the wider population with micro-ATM technology at lower costs. Furthermore, some of the recent success stories have claimed that the use of the Aadhaar card has resulted in ending identity fraud in entitlement schemes—the Mahatma Gandhi National Rural Employment Guarantee Act scheme (MGNREGA), and old age and widow pension schemes for women and men.

Enrolment

In June 2014, the Aadhaar enrolment reached a total of 63,65,07,332 individuals in the country having a gender breakdown of 47.99 per cent women (30,54,59,869 individuals), 51.99 per cent men (33,09,20,162 individuals) and a 0.2 per cent transgenders (1,27,301 individuals). Region-wise, the states of Maharashtra and Andhra Pradesh figured with high enrolments, while Jharkhand acquired 11th rank in the Aadhaar enrolment.

Figure 1.1

Aadhaar by Age and Gender

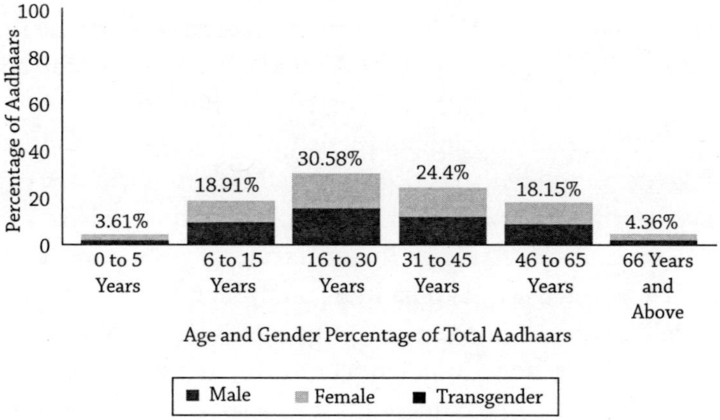

Source: *https://portal.uidai.gov.in/uidwebportal/dashboard.do* (accessed on 18 June 2014).

A sharp decline in Aadhaar enrolment since February 2014 may be interpreted on account of change in the government at the centre.

Biometric Identification System

A biometric identification system has two identity-related purposes: (i) It can identify an individual to see whether she/he is unique (Who is she/he?). This is a form of 1:N matching, where N

Figure 1.2

Aadhaar Trend

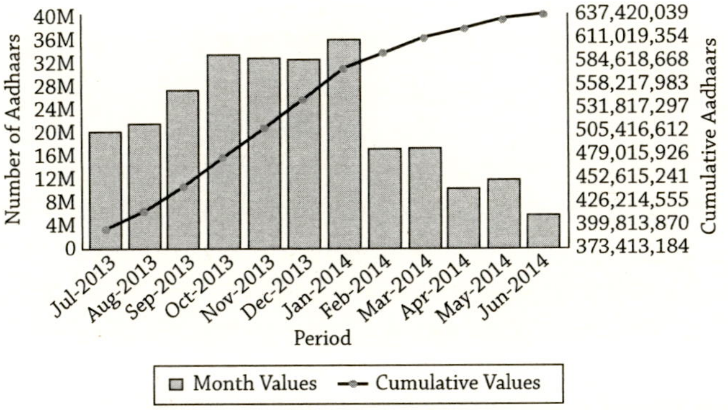

Source: https://portal.uidai.gov.in/uidwebportal/dashboard.do (accessed on 18 June 2014).

is the total number of persons in the biometric record; (ii) it can authenticate an individual (Is she who she claims to be?), i.e., provide a 1:1 matching.

As mentioned before, Aadhaar, a biometric identification system, is based on fingerprints and iris measurements. In addition to these, photographs are taken for 'biometric exceptions', i.e., those who, like manual workers, do not have recognisable fingerprints or whose irises cannot be measured. For such exceptions, photographs are used for visual verification. In the UID's analysis of 84 million cases, the total biometric failure was 0.14 per cent, which were then photographed (Zelazny, 2012: 16).

Since Aadhaar has not 1 but 12 data points, the probability of false rejections goes down drastically. For the 84 million cases analysed, the false rejection rate was just 0.057 per cent (Zelazny, 2012: 17).

The other type of problem is of false acceptance, i.e., when a person with duplicate entries is not detected. Again, the large number of data points along with the triple computer system led to a very low rate of 'false accepts' of just 0.0353 per cent. With India's population of 1.2 billion, this would give a potential of just 4,23,000 undetected duplicates (Zelazny, 2012).

A similar exercise has not been carried out for authentication, i.e., what number of enrolled people failed to be identified at the point of service. This could be done only when there are sufficient numbers being provided Aadhaar-based services.

Before India's Aadhaar scheme, many Latin American countries had biometric identification cards. But those were based on single identification points, i.e., single fingerprints; which could lead to many exclusions,for example, those with undistinguishable fingerprints. After the Aadhaar experience, many countries are now shifting to multiple identification points, which reduces the risk of exclusion. In addition, it is necessary to design a system to take care of exceptions i.e. for cases without adequate biometric measurements as the Aadhaar system does with photographs.

Women's Independent Identity with Aadhaar

Feminist analyses over the past several decades have shown that gender identities and social norms that define such identities emerge from traditional institutions and patriarchal power relations in a given social system. Women are trapped in traditional identification through family relations, as against men who distinctively display identification through market work rather than relationships. Such identification results in the invisibility of women's work and accords a secondary place to them in development analysis. Social norms are considered a far more powerful factor in determining the allocation of assets, productive/unproductive tasks and status rather than rational consideration of equality and efficiency.

The feminist questioning in the recent decades has forced a change in the conventional economic views and suggested the need to capture the complexity of factors that hide women's disadvantage in exercising their autonomy and agency within households and access to markets and public services (Bourdieu, 2001; Duflo 2012; Folbre, 1994; Kelkar, 2013). There is a need to change the norms that tend to shape and reinforce the gendered social structures, and power relations between women and men. Thus, even when policies for gender equality and women empowerment are launched, little results have been achieved in practice and implementation of such policies.

An enabling technological identity for individuals must benefit and empower all individuals, women and men. An identity that benefits women but does not empower them to make their own decisions over the use of their labour and assets places a potential barrier against the autonomy of women and their better life. Perhaps it would be useful to think of technological innovations such as Aadhaar as fitting into a social innovation that adopts an approach to make changes that radically transform gendered social inequalities and restructure arrangements in ways that will empower women with their autonomous identity and agency (as against considering women as the subordinate members of the household under the authority of the head of the household who are mostly men) and substantially shift the balance of power between women and men.

The major objectives of the present study are to assess whether Aadhaar has an impact on increasing women's independent identity and entitlement to public services, and on changing existing patriarchal social norms; and to provide policy assistance for improvement and increased efficiency with Aadhaar technology for gender equality.

Identity is used for a wide variety of pecuniary and nonpecuniary purposes, from income generation to concerns over status, inclusion and equal treatment. Furthermore, it is increasingly being recognised that what people care about and the extent of such care depends largely on their identity. It is in this context that we decided to undertake a collaborative multidisciplinary exploration of the UID scheme, with particular focus on the interaction of gender identity and Aadhaar technology for the improvement of women, i.e., increased autonomy and enhanced agency. Hence, a relevant question would be whether Aadhaar technology enhances women's capability to express, develop and realise their autonomy and agency in management of assets, including their dignity over their own physical assets and labour.

Based on the above discussion, the following two questions were identified as matters of empirical study in the two states of India: Jharkhand and Andhra Pradesh.

1. The nature of women's identity in a village—to what extent has an individual identity been established for women? In what spheres of social activity? Public (governmental, market-related); private (household, village)?

2. The nature and extent of the services that women can directly access such as direct benefit transfers, public distribution system, bank accounts and other benefits such as buying a SIM card for a mobile phone for own use or proving their identity to the police and outsiders.

What, however, is the role of identity in development? We turn to this question.

2

Need for Identification

Aadhaar is an identity system, whereby every individual (including children above the age of five) will have a unique identity. Does such an 'official' identity have a role to play in the development of a country or is it a bureaucratic exercise to collect information about people, with the possible use (misuse) for bureaucratic control or political purpose?

Official identity determines an individual's right to access the formal institutions like government entities, employers and banks. Furthermore, biometric identities are unique in the sense that they can be used to link identifying numbers and other records. After an official identity has been recorded, women or men can authenticate their identities using their unique numbers or identifiers (Gelb and Clark, 2013). Recent advances in biometric identification in more than 50 countries (China, Brazil, Japan, Iran, Israel, Indonesia and a number of European countries) have broken down many barriers related to 'the identity gap' (Kainth, 2011).

Generally speaking, the industrialised countries have systems whereby official identity for most individuals is established at birth, and this birth certificate enables them to access rights to state and non-state services and opportunities. This, however, is not the case in many industrialising countries of Asia. According to a UNICEF analysis, in the year 2000, South Asia had the highest proportion (63%) of children not registered at birth, even higher than Sub-Saharan Africa (55%) (quoted in Gelb and Clark, 2013: 7). As one would expect, under-registration is highly correlated with income and rural status. The poor in rural areas would be the most under-registered. In India, approximately 26 million births take place in a year, of which close to 14 million are registered; implying a non registration figure as high as 45 per cent, though there is a considerable variation in the level of registration in rural and urban areas (*http://unstats.un.org/unsd/vitalstatkb/attachment480.aspx*).

As UNICEF observes in its Public Policy Issue paper, *Birth Registration and Children* (UNICEF, 2007), "The right to identity consists in the legal and social acknowledgement of a person as a holder of rights and responsibilities, as well as the acknowledgement of his or her belonging to a country, a territory, a society and a family"—an essential condition for preserving a person's individual and collective dignity. Lack of such identity (be it in the form of a card or a verifiable number) makes an individual invisible in the eyes of society and state machinery; and without it, he/she would risk not being able to access diverse public and private services.

Since birth registration and consequently the birth certificate constitutes the first and the most direct way for an individual to get a legal identity and enter the official state machinery, this lack of registration results in the difficulty (and often impossibility) of the unregistered children (and adults, if this situation of lack of documentation is not rectified at a later moment in their lives) to access basic public services, thus locking them in a vicious circle of marginalisation and vulnerability. The lack of an official identity, a document or a number that allows an individual to prove who she/he is in her/his interactions with state and non-state actors and service providers, can adversely and severely affect many aspects of her/his day to day and strategic transactions.

An official identity is often required when an individual approaches a state entity to access basic services such as free or subsidised healthcare and education. Those who need such public services the most are the individuals belonging to the most, economically and socially, marginalised sections of the society; the very individuals who tend not to have valid official IDs. Turned away by public service providers, often, the only alternative that such individuals have is to either not access those services or try to access private services, which often they are unable to afford, thus throwing them into a debt cycle. Thus even though, apparently, the state provides equal basic services for all, its failure to provide valid legal identity to sections of its citizens or to the individuals residing within its territory, essentially, renders these services inaccessible or of little use to those who need them the most.

Same is the case with the social security and welfare benefits such as pensions, scholarships, food subsidies, health insurance and other poverty reduction schemes provided by a government for its most marginalised people. The programmes may be there, but the fact that those who are entitled to these programmes are often not legally 'identified' excludes them from enjoying the benefits of the programmes. Similarly, the lack of proper official identification systems makes it very difficult for a government to monitor that those who eventually receive these benefits are really the ones who are entitled.

A bank account (and bank credit) often allows an individual to embark on a positive path of economic development both by saving and investing own resources, and by leveraging a credit facility at favourable rates to invest in own education, business project etc. However, banks like most other state and non-state actors require their potential clients to have an official identity. Thus, individuals who lack such identification are mostly the women; a great majority of them have no property in their independent names and thus lack rights to access credit from financial institutions. They remain at the margins of the formal financial system and are forced to resort to informal mechanisms such as local moneylenders, exposing them to exorbitant rates of interest on credits, exploitative loan conditions, risk to their savings and investment, etc. In case of families and individuals with migrant members who regularly send and receive remittances to their hometown/village, the impossibility of holding a bank account implies higher costs and risks in the process of remittance transfers.

Thus, official identity is usually a prerequisite for an individual in participating with full rights in a country´s legal, political and economic system through voting, becoming a candidate for elective office, pursuing a case in a legal court of justice, getting legally married, buying, selling and inheriting property, running a business in her/his own name, finding formal employment, etc.

Often to overcome such situations that arise out of lack of official identity, these marginalised and 'invisible' individuals are forced to pay bribes to unscrupulous public employees or other private individuals acting as intermediaries between the official machinery and those whose existence does not figure in the system, in order to get some kind of 'official identity'. This not only foments corruption in the system, but also makes these unregistered citizens even more vulnerable and dependent on other more powerful sections of the population. Such problems are of course not usually faced by economically richer sections of the population as they usually have some (or various) forms of identification and in case of lack of it, sufficient resources (monetary, information or influence) to obtain such identity.

Thus the lack of a well-functioning universal official identification system in a country, serves to perpetuate the marginalisation, vulnerability and poverty of the 'unidentified', reinforces inequality between the different social classes, and more generally acts as an obstacle to the country´s economic, social and political development. Recognising these and other problems that arise from the lack of a systematic and universal system of official identification, many developing countries are working to put in place mechanisms by which all individuals residing in their territories have access to an identity card/number through which they can effectively access their other fundamental rights.

In India, this role is sought to be played by the Aadhaar or the UID number. Aadhaar is being widely discussed in terms of the role it will play in different applications such as in facilitating cash transfers, but it is imperative not to lose sight of the fact that the key attribute of Aadhaar is precisely the universal identity infrastructure that it lays down in a country as 'under-documented' and as large and complex as India.

Official Identification such as Aadhaar confers a personal identity on an individual. This personal identity goes against the norms of many traditional cultures, where women are often referred to and known by their relations to others rather than by their own identities.

A relational identity maybe adequate within localised and community-based interactions. But when matters of the state are concerned, then a non-relational individual identity, one which is amenable to third party verification, is required. State officials require such a non-relational identity for keeping records, providing benefits and collecting taxes. The identity needs to be unique, so that a person can be clearly identified and is not mixed with another.

Aadhaar based personal identity should be distinguished from social identity, which is based on a person's affiliations with social groups. Affiliations with social groups include not only caste or community, but also profession and a host of other affiliations that one may choose. These, as Sen (2009) emphasises, can change over time, but personal identity does not. Personal identity, however, does not exist in just one manner. As pointed out here, personal identity can be individualised or relational. Aadhaar introduces the process of shifting from relational to individualised personal identity.

Individualised personal identity is much more of a problem for poor women than it is for poor men. Both poor women and poor men could have problems in establishing their identities due to lack of documentation. But in various development schemes and government entitlements, men are individually recognised and acknowledged as 'head of household'. Women remain subsumed under the category of household members—socially and administratively.

In India, the traditional means that women (more so in the rural areas and among poorer sections of the population) had of accessing most state services was through the PDS (public distribution system) card, also known as the ration card. This card, traditionally used not only for accessing subsidised food but also used as a general means of identification in various spheres of public life (both for state and non-state services) was issued to the family as a whole in the name of the head of the household (mostly a male), thus rendering the women members of the household dependent on the male household head for access to basic services or other needs of identification. For the purpose of government service delivery, the universal PDS (family based) card was followed by a more targeted system of subsidies through the so called Below Poverty Line or BPL card, which was also family based and did not take individual identity into consideration. One type of individual identity card (for both women and men) is widespread even in the rural areas of the country. This is the voter ID card, which entitles the holders to exercise their basic political right of voting as individuals. However, the economic entitlements as mentioned above continue to be governed by the underlying emphasis on a unique social (family) identity. The new Aadhaar card, however, is intended to be universally accepted; so it will better contribute to build multidimensional social identities, importantly identities that will contribute to the economic empowerment of women.

3

Women's Autonomous Identity and Agency

The question of identity is that of who one is. This includes a name but goes beyond that to aspects of existence, an existence that is always social and autonomous (as against relational and dependent). To amend the poet John Donne, "No woman is an island, entire unto herself". A woman may identify herself by what she does—whether she is a wage worker, a professional, a homemaker, etc. As Sen (2009) points out, we all have multiple identities and we may at any point stress one or the other of those identities (e.g., being a Hindu or a Muslim, or being a wage labourer or a professional, etc.).

However, what does identity entail? Using the domain of gender as an example, there is, first of all, an identification of a person as a woman or a man, or as a girl or a boy. Being a woman means what she does/does not do. There is a conventional, traditional element involved here, as it were, that informs a girl/woman what she should do/not do. These are the norms that determine how one should behave in different situations. Norms may be explicit or implicit (in many countries women have been required by law to change their names on marriage), but may carry the force of the weight of tradition, what Bourdieu (2001) terms as doxa or received traditional norms. When a couple, both working, return home from work, who goes to the kitchen and who sits down to relax or watch television? There is a norm about this and similar behaviour, and it is these norms that form the basis of the gender categories of women and men.

The norm then results in or influences the behaviour of women and men in different situations. Of course, there can be changes in norms, whether in a couple, in many households or in the society as a whole. How such changes in norms come about is the subject of inquiry itself, and we propose to look at how Aadhaar could possibly contribute to changing the existing norms of gendered behaviour.

At this point, however, what is necessary to point out is that gender categories, norms and behaviour all constitute identity in a way that even economists have begun to recognise. Discussing how norms affect economic behaviour and choice of gender identity in labour market relations, Akerlof and Kranton in their recent study (2010) conclude that men do not generally dislike working with women. Their dislike is job specific, for example, women as secretaries and men as executives. Therefore,

- Women invest in skills for jobs that are appropriate for women (education rather than business schooling or engineering).
- Women may have a lower attachment to the labour force because of wider fender norms (women are expected to stay home and raise children).
- The real problem is the norms that regulate that women and men should do particular jobs, irrespective of their individual tastes and abilities.

Furthermore, whatever gains have come up as a result of the feminist critique of labour market relations and of conventional economic interpretations of work, they are likely to be at risk with the new form of women's incorporation in global production systems.

Taking gender identity as constituting an interrelated set of gender categories (women and men), norms (what each gender is supposed to do or not do) and behaviour (what each gender does or does not do), what does Aadhaar do to change it or strengthen it? The first point is that Aadhaar allows a woman to be recognised by her own name, something that does not occur in traditional societies in India. This in itself is a breaking of the traditional norm wherein a woman is known by her relationship to her husband (*malkin*, meaning wife of the owner/landowner; or *panditain* or *thakurain*, meaning wife of the male householder in a Brahmin or Thakur family; *gharwali*, meaning wife of the householder) or her relationship to her son (mother of so and so), etc.

A public policy for an independent identity for a woman to be known in social and economic spheres is then the first rupture with tradition that Aadhaar brings about. Of course, it should be pointed out that Aadhaar is not the first instrument for such public recognition of a woman's own identity. The voter identity card or the Smart Card, widely used in Andhra Pradesh, are also similarly based on a woman's own name and confer a public recognition of that name.

Aadhaar provides a foundational identity for a woman. What else happens with that identity depends on what it is used for. It can, for instance, be used for transfer of cash benefits or Direct Benefit Transfers (DBTs), as it is called in India. In directly providing such benefits to a woman, and not through a man (husband or son), Aadhaar provides autonomy to a woman, i.e., the freedom to ask for her entitlements (from the state) and the consequent ability to determine her own actions as well as manage her own resources, however limited they might be. Of course, there are social norms about such freedoms, stressing that a woman should not decide herself about how to spend money. But such norms are buttressed by the fact that women do not have their own money or assets. When women have to ask men for money, then there is not much they can do about being autonomous decision-makers. But when women are accorded an independent identity and given money of their own, as in the case of old age/widowhood/disability pensions provided directly to women, then they have the possibility of being able to realise their autonomy.

The second step that Aadhaar makes possible is that of agency for women. Since cash benefits in the name of women are transferred directly to them, they can assert their say and action in deciding on how to spend that money. This would enable them to acquire power over economic decisions and asset management that influence their lives and status in society. What this means is that the money directly transferred to women could be used by them in line with their own priorities and decisions. For instance, old women could, with their pensions, decide on buying medicines for themselves and not depend on the uncertain benevolence of their sons. The use of autonomy provided by direct transfer of benefits to women could result in behaviour that is at variance with the existing norms and in line with women's own priorities. This is the exercise of agency, the capacity to make and act on one's own choices. Such agency could extend to other non-monetary benefits such as the ability to use the Aadhaar card to buy a SIM card.

Autonomy and agency can be applied in many spheres of social activity. When applied together in the sphere of economic activity, the result can be called economic empowerment: namely, the ability to choose and act on one's choices in the economic sphere, as in buying or selling in the market, owning and managing assets, being employed, etc. For women, gaining these capabilities itself goes against the existing norms of women's social-economic subordination.

Figure 3.1

Aadhaar Identity and Empowerment Process

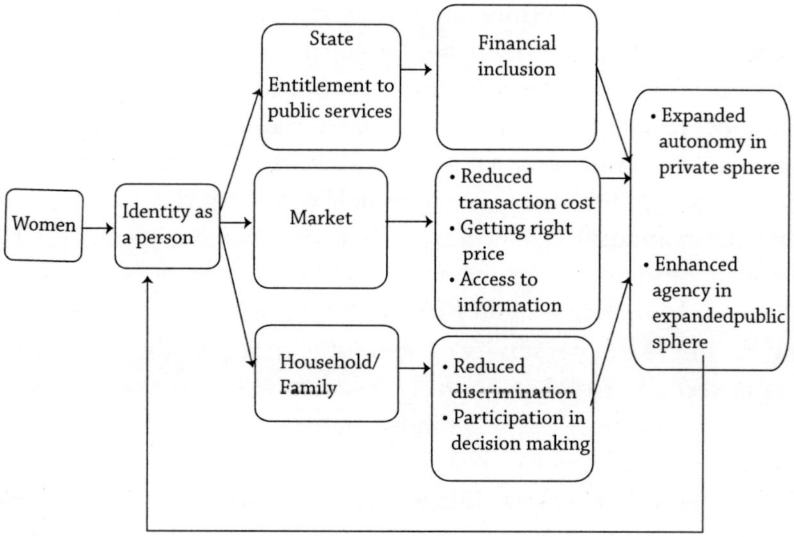

Aadhaar identity has the potential to reinforce the empowerment effects on women. It establishes citizenship relation with the state and augments access to public services, and the state's welfare and development programmes. Women with individual identity access and negotiate with markets and advance towards overcoming traditionally imposed limits on their mobility and negotiating/bargaining skills. The outcome of this process is getting control over resources which may lead to improvement in autonomy, both within the household and also in social spaces; which, in turn, could lead to enhanced status of women within the household and increased autonomy and agency in addressing their concerns with the state and the market (Figure 3.1).

Empowerment, however, is not a one-step achievement. There are many steps to such empowerment. For instance, take the case of a single woman. For her, the steps to empowerment include getting enough money to buy her own medicines, having some more to be able to give small presents, having enough to contribute for her own food in the household, being able to contribute for more than her own food, or owning the house in which the household resides.

Going through each one of these steps has two sides to it. There is the necessity of assertion by women and there is the possibility of resistance by men. Even at the stage of merely establishing an identity in a name card, men may question why there is any need for such an identity, when they are there to provide an identity for the whole household. Similarly, the direct transfer of benefits may also be opposed. Even more likely is opposition when women try to utilise their money in ways that go against community norms. For instance, in Jharkhand, where women do often have some of their own money from sale of non-timber forest products (NTFP) or wage labour, there is the norm that they should spend this only on household needs and not use any of it for herself or her parents. This kind of norm exists even in Hindu and other communities. But among the Oraon tribe in Jharkhand, any violation of this norm could result in the woman being denounced as a witch. What is to be noted is that each step of empowerment requires assertion by women in view of the potential resistance by men.

4

Aadhaar Implementation in Andhra Pradesh

This study was conducted in two districts in Andhra Pradesh: Ranga Reddy and East Godavari. These two districts fall into the first phase of districts selected for Aadhaar implementation: Ranga Reddy, Hyderabad, Chittoor, Anantapur and East Godavari. Prior to the Aadhaar-enabled Payments System (AEPS), the biometric system of payments through the smart card has been in vogue since 2008. Ranga Reddy district is yet to start its public service delivery through the AEPS, whereas East Godavari district is implementing the AEPS with regard to the following schemes: Social Security Payment (SSP), Mahatma Gandhi National Rural Employment Guarantee Scheme (MGNREGS), student scholarships, Janani Suraksha Yojana (JSY) and the public distribution system (PDS). Since these schemes were not rolled out throughout the district, the *mandals* (with specific schemes) that rolled out these schemes were selected for the study such as Thatiparthy village in Gollaprolu Mandal where essential commodities were supplied through the AEPS; Penumarthy in Kakinada rural mandal was selected as SSP payments and MGNREGS payments were made through the AEPS. In order to capture the variations in the functioning of the AEPS, we also selected tribal mandal Rampachodavaram in East Godavari.

As the AEPS had not yet started in Ranga Reddy district, MGNREGS and social security payments were made through the smart card system. We selected three villages (Yacharam, Choudaripally and Nandivanaparthy) in Yacharam Mandal in Ranga Reddy district.

Separate focus group discussions (FGDs) were conducted with women and men in all the selected villages to capture their perceptions regarding: (i) their identity in the village; (ii) their awareness of and familiarity with the Aadhaar card; (iii) pre and post Aadhaar situations regarding women's access to and control of payments like MGNREGS, pensions, PDS ration and benefits under other schemes; (iv) women's increased presence and participation in private and public spaces; and (v) difficulties faced in the implementation of Aadhaar and how they could be addressed.

A total of 13 FGDs were conducted in the 7 villages selected for the field work. Of those, 7 FGDs were conducted with women and 6 with men. The number of participants in all the FGDs were 241, of which 44 per cent were men and 56 per cent were women. Average participants in 1 FGD were 18 people and average participants per village were 34.

Aadhaar-Enabled Payment Systems

People in Ranga Reddy district did not have a clear idea about the use of the Aadhaar card but they did know that it would be useful for multiple purposes like getting a connection for LPG, disbursal of ration from PDS shops, old age and widowhood pensions and MGNREGS wage payments. People in East Godavari, however, understand that Aadhaar is an individual identity (ID) card that is useful for obtaining the aforementioned benefits from the government and also non-government benefits such as opening of bank accounts and buying SIM cards for mobile phones.

Information on the Aadhaar card and its enrolment reached them through *dandora* (public announcement) and also through self-help groups (SHGs) in Yacharam mandal in Ranga Reddy district. In East Godavari, village meetings were conducted and the village revenue assistant (VRA) explained the usefulness of the Aadhaar identity. The SHGs and PDS dealers also supplied information. Women and men could access information on Aadhaar equally. Filled-in applications were submitted at the *gram panchayat* office or to the Aadhaar team for enrolment. According to the data collected through the FGDs, in Yacharam, 60 per cent of those enrolled received their Aadhaar cards; in Nandivanaparthy, 70 per cent received Aadhaar cards; and in Choudaripally, 90 per cent of the enrolled received their Aadhaar cards. Compared to women, men have more documents to prove their identity such as bank account passbooks, ration cards, and land registration *pattas* or title deeds. The anganwadi workers (AWWs) helped to complete the applications and submit them to the Aadhaar team/*gram panchayat* in East Godavari district. The civil supplies department has completed the process of seeding of Below Poverty Line (BPL) households. Seeding is a process whereby the unique identification (UID) is added to the database of beneficiaries. Each beneficiary, of say MGNREGS, PDS or pensions, is identified by a beneficiary number relevant to the scheme and the UID. As a result, the beneficiary database contains name, beneficiary identifier number and UID. The Commissioner (Registrar for UIDAI) Food and Civil Supplies has completed more than 30 million enrolments in the state.

Figure 4.1

A Woman Receiving Old Age Pension with AEPS in a Village in Andhra Pradesh

During our field study in East Godavari district in April 2013, enrolment was reported to have covered 99.53 per cent of the population and only 15,000 people were left to be covered by Aadhaar (GoAP, 2013). Our interviewees said that the process of enrolment was easy and simple. They however did say that enrolment in remote areas would be difficult for the elderly and the infirm people as mobility to the enrolment centre would be a problem.

Women and men generally found the process of filling out forms difficult and they required assistance to do so. It would be helpful if local officials could assist them in filling out the enrolment forms. Since Aadhaar did not have women employees in the district, the women expressed their preference for women officers in the process of enrolment. They further stated that they needed exclusive counters for their enrolment.

Enrolment of adults was given priority in Ranga Reddy district as pension disbursal was to be linked to the AEPS. In the current phase, LPG holders and students are being enrolled on a priority basis since the government of Andhra Pradesh has planned to link subsidised cooking gas with Aadhaar-enabled services.

The problem of rough and erased finger-lines prevailed only in 5 to 10 per cent of people, mostly above 50 years of age. They had to reapply for the issue of the Aadhaar card. Problems in delivery of Aadhaar identity cards are due to insufficient enrolment centres and many of the centres being located at considerable distance from the village, delayed generation of identity cards and no assistance in completing necessary procedures. Additionally, erased finger-lines, especially for the very old, and iris scan for people who had undergone cataract surgery were also responsible for the failure to enrol for Aadhaar cards.

In East Godavari district, the AEPS is in place. Under the AEPS developed by the National Payment Corporation of India, a person holding the Aadhaar number can carry out financial transactions using the micro ATM provided by the local business correspondent. The Aadhaar card was used for varied purposes like buying a SIM card for a mobile phone, opening a bank account, booking an LPG (cooking gas) cylinder, obtaining a driver's licence or caste certificates and admission of school children into a government school (Table 5.2). However, in the tribal village of Peddageddada in Rampachodavaram, all payments were made through the smart card. Though Aadhaar cards have been issued in Rampachodavaram (tribal) Mandal and the

Aadhaar database has been created, the AEPS is still not in place due to discontinuous power supply and weak internet connectivity. Also, MGNREGS payments were made manually by the community service provider (CSP) and pensions were paid through smart cards. The case of South coastal districts with high human development, gender development and gender empowerment (values falling into a narrow band) can be explained in terms of consistent economic growth, high female literacy, favourable female and child sex ratios, high sex ratio in enrolment, and high political participation and low work participation; in short, as traditionally developed region. Historically, coastal Andhra had the favourable effect of having assured irrigation and early onset of green revolution, which has led to consistent agricultural and agriculture-based industrial growth. All these changes have tightened the labour market also resulting in rise in wages and reduction in the gender wage gap (Revathi, 1998).

Another favourable factor in case of south coastal districts is the customary practice of giving land to women by the natal family at the time of marriage. Though this is confined to land owning upper caste categories (especially the Kamma), there is evidence that the practice has percolated to land owning middle order castes too (Revathi, 2012). The state amendment of Hindu Succession Act (HSA) of 1956 by the Andhra Pradesh government in 1986 also can be seen as a positive move where women as coparceners could legally obtain an equal share in family property. Another important issue that could have a favourable impact on women's economic empowerment is the Dalit women's migration to Middle East countries from East Godavari district as house maids and care givers.[1] They could accumulate assets like house and also send their children to higher (technical) education. Hence, gender relations are more favourable to women where they have more control on income and hence more say in decision-making at the household level.

In Ranga Reddy district, in the selected villages, smart card (an offline payment system) was used for delivery of all schemes. There is

1. Women belonging mostly to scheduled caste began migrating to Saudi Arabia and other middle east countries in the 1970s especially from Razole

a technical service provider (TSP) who is the business correspondent (BC) who provides the service. The TSP (also sometimes outsourced to an NGO) has a three-layered network—the district coordinator (DC), the *mandal* coordinator (MC) and the CSP. The authentication of the beneficiary is made through the smart card, which links to the local server. This is a local verification. Six fingerprints are enrolled and if any of those does not match, there is a provision for manual payment.

The MCs upload the data after every payment session and also install the updated version into the computers of the CSPs. The CSPs are given one per cent as commission and there is no fixed salary for this work. The government gives two per cent commission of which one per cent is given to the CSPs and the other one per cent is shared by the banks and the TSP. Further, the CSPs are insured for ₹ 2,00,000 in case of theft or loss of money. They are not insured for any physical injury sustained during the time of their assigned work. The AEPS has not been introduced in Ranga Reddy district yet but for entry identification, the Aadhaar card or the enrolment identity (EID) are being used. EID is a 14-digit acknowledgement slip of enrolment for the Aadhaar card and it contains the enrolment ID, and the date and time stamp. It is used for tracking the issue of UID to the resident.

In most FGDs, it was said that Aadhaar is equally important for both women and men. For women, Aadhaar is useful for obtaining loans and cooking gas connections, opening bank accounts, getting scholarships for girls and accessing the Janani Suraksha Yojna (JSY) benefits (for pregnant women). In 1999, the government of Andhra Pradesh had launched the Deepam scheme by which one million LPG connections were issued to women from BPL households in rural areas. All the beneficiaries were members of Development of Women and Children in Rural Areas (DWCRA) groups. Now women would receive the direct cash benefit as the reimbursement of the subsidised cost of cooking gas. Women as mothers of minor students who are eligible for scholarships from the government would receive these benefits through joint accounts along with their children.

Unlike in the case of Jharkhand, Aadhaar cards of all family members were kept in safe custody mostly by the women. The women

Table 4.1

Delivery of Public Services in Selected Villages

			Delivery Mode of Public Services				
District	*Mandal*	*Village*	*NREGS*	*Pension*	*Scholarships*	*PDS*	*Other Uses*
East Godavari	Kakinada rural	Penumarthy	AEPS	AEPS	AEPS		Bank account Cooking gas, SIM card
	Gollaprolu	Thatiparthy	Post office	Smart card	AEPS	AEPS	Bank account Cooking gas, SIM card
	Rampacho davaram	Peddageddada	Manual	Smart card and manual	SHG based village organisation leader		Bank account Cooking gas, SIM card, Caste certificate, Admission to schools
		Chinnageddada	Manual	Smart card and manual	Aadhaar and Manual		Bank account Cooking gas, SIM card
Ranga Reddy	Yacharam	Yacharam, Choudaripally Nandivana parthy	Smart card	Smart card			Bank account Cooking gas, SIM card and Caste certificate

carried their Aadhaar cards when they went to the market, hospital/primary health centre or even to the SHG meetings.

Women in the Yacharam village in Ranga Reddy district were of the opinion that the Aadhaar card would be a substitute for a number of cards currently used for specific purposes. They said that Aadhaar would be more beneficial to women as it would enable them to receive all benefits from the government directly.

From the various uses of the Aadhaar card, it appears that the state is enforcing a demand-driven system by linking the Aadhaar identity to various utilities both public and market based, and making it a multipurpose national identification system even though the Aadhaar identity is not mandated for accessing some of these utilities.

Aadhaar in the Context of Gender Relations

Gender is a fundamental dimension of stratification in society and exists in every sphere of human activity, in households, and public spaces/institutions (state, market and civil society). Unequal gender relations imply that men not only have and can exercise greater power than women in almost all spheres of functioning; but they also have culturally and often legally sanctioned power over women, and greater control of and access to resources and information. Gender relations are shaped by a number of factors like the structural (historical); institutional; socioeconomic and cultural development levels and legality. Structural changes may have been effected by state by itself or prompted by social movements by different sections of people.

The government of Andhra Pradesh has provided a larger space for women SHGs in its strategy to alleviate poverty and empower women. This is visible in the women's groups promoted under the South Asia Poverty Alleviation Programme (SAPAP) with suitable improvements to develop and implement the Andhra Pradesh District Poverty Initiatives Project (APDPIP) and the Andhra Pradesh Rural Poverty Reduction Project (APRPRP) (Galab and Chandrasekhar, 2003). Later the programme, earlier called Velugu or SERP (Society for Elimination of Poverty) and presently known as Indira Kranthi Patham or the IKP, was scaled up to cover the entire state. The SERP has begun the social mobilisation of women through SHGs for their collective empowerment. The SERP, with a network of SHGs under a federal architecture, was able to design and implement over a period of time as many as 18 programmes under the banner of IKP, for the benefit of the poor. As a result, women have experienced advancement in their status within the household and in public spaces.

According to IKP, the overall long-term rural poverty reduction programme objective is to help enable the poor to overcome poverty through a holistic approach of facilitating and promoting empowerment, creating opportunities, providing mechanism for social security and working for equity. IKP has achieved poverty reduction milestones on multiple dimensions. It has made rapid strides in not only membership and the institutions for poor women but also in activities like securing institutional credit, undertaking dairy, collective marketing, and initiatives like food security, social security, health and nutrition during the period 2000-01 to 2010-11.

A number of SHG women are included in the delivery system in the case of social security payments (pensions) as CSPs, with functions to deliver old age/widow/physically handicapped pensions, MGNREGS wages, stipends and scholarships. Besides, SHGs have become centres of information for the women regarding any new programme taken up by the government. Against this backdrop of a pre-existing empowerment process, it can be said that Aadhaar identity has further advanced the empowerment effects experienced by women.

As the programme for organising women into SHGs has been in place for a long time and it has contributed to their social empowerment, it is now considered a benchmark for looking at the issues of women's identity, empowerment effects and patriarchal norms within the household and in the society at large.

In a number of cases, women SHG members said that in order to facilitate their participation in SHG activities, the men have transformed their attitudes towards sharing the gendered household work and taking care of children. According to their statements, household violence has also reduced compared to before.

Figure 4.2

A Woman Receiving Widow Pension with AEPS in a Village in Andhra Pradesh

Women in most FGDs stated that the reason for this increased respect is due to their ability to repay debts and provide an additional income to the household. Many women have come to be recognised in public spaces like banks by their own name. They also have learned to negotiate in public spaces. Women from indigenous villages (in Rampachodavaram) also said that they could go to the market and banks independently.

Notwithstanding the above, patriarchal norms are still strong in terms of identifying women in the village. With the exception of indigenous women, in the rest of the study villages, it was said that women were mostly identified by the family name and/or by their natal village. They were not identified by their own names and children were identified by the father's name.

Women's capacity to earn cash is at par with the men in indigenous villages. In the general situation, women even earn more than the men. This is true in 15 to 25 per cent of all households in the study area. Women in around 25 to 75 per cent households earn equal to men across all selected villages. Cash earnings of men are spent after consultation with women. In the case of Yacharam in Ranga Reddy, this however, was not the case and women had to account for expenses to the men. In case of non-compliance, there would be a fight and physical violence. The matter gets aggravated if women refuse to give money for alcohol. While women have some autonomy regarding daily consumption needs and petty expenses, the permission of the husband is required in case of bigger expenditure items. Hence, male control over financial decisions remains high.

Surprisingly, if a woman has a regular job and the husband does not have one, then it is not a cause of embarrassment to the man and there would be no damage to the family status. Women's autonomy and agency would be increased in such cases. The response of men in such situations is mixed across the villages. In villages in East Godavari, men do not bother even if a woman earns more than them. But in Ranga Reddy villages, the situation is vastly different and there the women said that the men cannot digest a situation where a woman earns more. Even where women were working and earning at par or more than the man of the house, the man would not share housework. Unlike in Ranga Reddy, in East Godavari villages, the men would help in household work. It is to be noted that the gendered household work would change occasionally, when a woman is sick. The question is whether the Aadhaar identity has brought about any change in this area.

Women's Identity and Empowerment

Women's identity is generally derived from the identity of her husband or her father. The Aadhaar identity gives women an individual identity of their own, which entails freedom and power for them. The men agree with the women's perception that due to women's earnings, household incomes have been augmented and that this additional income is largely used for providing family members with better food, clothing, health care and schooling of children. Importantly, physical violence on women is much less and some men have begun sharing housework and taking care of the children when their wives attend the SHG meetings. Approximately 15 to 25 per cent women earn more than men, as we noted in Penumarthy and Thatiparthy villages of East

Godavari; but in Yacharam and Choudaripally villages of Ranga Reddy district, only 5 to 10 per cent women earned more than men. This shows women's relatively better position in East Godavari, because of their better earning capacity. The onset of high yielding varieties (HYV) in agricultural technology in the 1960s till the 1980s has tightened the labour market and resulted in a rise in general wage levels and reduction in gender disparity in agricultural wages (Revathi, 1998). Secondly, women's migration to the Middle East countries as domestic helpers and hospital attendants has reportedly also contributed to the economic independence of women, which has led them to purchase assets like land and houses in their own names.

With regard to institutional support, the process of obtaining identity cards like the voter ID card or the PDS card was relatively smooth for the women in Penumarthy and Thatiparthy villages in East Godavari. In Ranga Reddy district, the women faced a number of problems like inordinate delay, 'speed money' (bribe), lack of knowledge and ability to pursue procedures, hence their dependency on others.

All the men interviewed agreed without a single dissenting voice that the women have to account for both income and expenditure to their husbands. Admittedly, there is violence within the households, largely because of alcoholism among the men and the growing assertion by women. Women's earnings more than their husbands was not considered an issue; it was instead seen as an input that helped improve the family's status. As reported in East Godavari, there were a few men who would share housework and they were not seen as the odd man out. However, these men still remained as 'helpers' in housework, doing limited work such as fetching water, firewood and taking care of children. All this shows that the norm of attending to housework by men has been accepted to some extent. The men admitted that women are not weak and that they have grown stronger because of being members of SHGs; and that the SHG women are stronger and cleverer than other women.

Women are in control of the benefits received by them and they tend to use these resources for the education and nutritional needs of their children. However, they find themselves weaker and vulnerable than men due to lack of schooling or literacy.

There were women in our FGDs who said that they had not faced any problem due to lack of identification documents in general as almost everyone in the village either had a voter identity card or a BPL card. But there were women who did not have a ration card, such as migrants and newly married women, and they faced problems in receiving MGNREGS payments and also in opening bank accounts. For example, in all the villages in Ranga Reddy district, there were women who had no proper identification document and hence could not receive pensions, PDS benefits or access loans and other benefits from the government schemes. Those women stated that there would be no recognition for them outside the household if they did not have an identity card of their own. Ration cards are mostly in the name of the men as head of household and women therefore have no independent personal access to housing, agricultural land, housing plots, bank loans, MGNREGS job card, etc.

The opposition from the men in Ranga Reddy to women's individual identity and assertion as a result of government initiatives was not found among the men in East Godavari. In the latter district, the men saw it as 'benefitting the household' and not as being divisive within the household. This may be due to the relatively stronger patriarchal hold in Ranga Reddy which is reflected in the low gender empowerment measure index (GEM) for the region of South Telangana compared to the high value of the index for south coastal Andhra, which comprises the East Godavari district. The Ranga Reddy district ranks seventh in GEM while East Godavari ranks second in the state (GoAP and CESS, 2007).

Seeds of change in gender relations could be observed due to the multidimensional changes taking place, especially the state's initiative to empower women by addressing them as economic agents. Given this favourable institutional backdrop, it is more probable for them to access information on any new initiative if not to wield greater power than men. We found in the study on Aadhaar that women obtained information about the project through SHGs and even got enrolled through Mandal Samakhyas. Besides, women also are working as community service providers for many social security programmes.

5

Aadhaar Implementation in Jharkhand

Aadhaar Project in the State

A Memorandum of Understanding (MoU) was signed between the Unique Identity Authority of India (UIDAI) and the Government of Jharkhand (GoJH) on 25 June 2010 to implement the UID project in Jharkhand with the objective of enhancing the efficiency in delivery of government benefits and services through accurate identification of beneficiaries, and to have uniform standards and processes for verification and identification of beneficiaries. For this purpose, the government of Jharkhand set up a state level empowered committee under the chairpersonship of the Governor of Jharkhand and a state-level UID implementation committee under the chairmanship of the chief secretary of Jharkhand to oversee the implementation of UID in the state.

In 2011, the GoJH decided to undertake a Financial Inclusion and Welfare Payments pilot project in 12 blocks. The districts that served as pioneers in the implementation of this pilot were Ranchi (Ratu block), Saraikela-Kharsawan (Chandil block), Ramgarh (Ramgarh block) and Hazaribagh (Hazaribagh, Sadar block).

The first service to be covered by the Aadhaar-enabled payment system (AEPS) was the payment of Mahatma Gandhi National Rural Employment Guarantee Act scheme (MGNREGA) wages, followed by social security pensions and scholarships. The banks involved at this stage in the experiment were Bank of India, ICICI Bank and Union Bank of India. Business Correspondents (BCs) with micro ATMs (costing less than ₹ 20,000, weighing less than 2 kg, linked to a laptop and supported by four to six hours of power backup) were deployed at the *panchayat* level for the disbursement of payments. The first transaction was carried out in December 2011 and was soon followed by 2,222 more successful transactions for disbursing a total amount of ₹ 1,87,482 (UIDAI, 2012), thus making Jharkhand the first state in the country to make MGNREGS payments through Aadhaar-based bank accounts. In October 2012, the deputy commissioner of Ramgarh was given the Aadhaar governance award for exemplary implementation of Aadhaar-linked MGNREGS payments in the district.

However, the implementation of the UID pilot in Jharkhand in 2012 was not without its problems. Even as the project was 'adopted' and strongly supported by the state chief minister, right from the outset, in February 2012, Aadhaar enrolment was temporarily suspended for want of funds. Another problem faced by UID implementation in the state was the delayed start and slow enrolment in some rural areas.

The second phase of Aadhaar enrolment by UIDAI and the Aadhaar-enabled payment of government-sponsored socio-economic schemes, including MGNREGS, started in Jharkhand in the third week of April 2012. After the initial experiments with the MGNREGS, pensions and scholarship payments in 2012, the state government proposed that the salaries and pensions of government employees be paid using their UID numbers. However, due to low coverage of enrolments among government employees, this proposal could not be implemented. This decision was reiterated in May 2013 and all government employees were asked to enrol for Aadhaar by 31 August 2013 (*The Pioneer*, 2013a).

In keeping with the central government's introduction of Direct Benefit Transfers (DBT) in 43 districts (later increased to 78) in the country in 2013, in Jharkhand, too, further impetus was given to Aadhaar-based DBTs. Four districts (Ranchi, Ramgarh, Hazaribagh and Saraikela-Kharsawan) in the state were selected for this purpose. Since then, plans to link Aadhaar to DBTs in several government programmes (for example, scholarships, the Janani Suraksha Yojana [JSY], liquefied petroleum gas or LPG etc.) have been announced.

In April 2013, the human resource development department of Jharkhand directed the district superintendents of education (DSE) to ensure that every child is enrolled into Aadhaar by the end of the year (in April 2013, 65% of students studying in government schools in the state were already enrolled into UID) so that UID could be made mandatory for government school students in Jharkhand to avail the benefit of scholarship programmes (*http://egovreach.in/social/content/Aadhaar-card-mandatory-govt-school-students-jharkhand*). Apart from increasing the efficiency in the delivery of scholarships, providing each student with an individual Aadhaar number would also allow the government to obtain the exact figure of students, monitor the dropout rate and manage fund allocation for the midday meal scheme more effectively.

Aadhaar has also been made mandatory for availing LPG subsidy through DBT in Jharkhand's Hazaribagh district (Srivastava, 2013). Another step towards Aadhaar-linked DBTs in the state has been the decision to seed the bank accounts of JSY beneficiaries with their Aadhaar numbers in Ranchi district. To facilitate the beneficiaries' move to Aadhaar-linked DBTs, special Aadhaar enrolment camps have been proposed and those in charge of the primary health centres have been directed to help the women in opening their bank accounts. (*The Pioneer*, 2013b).

The latest application of Aadhaar announced by the GoJH has been in making the Aadhaar number mandatory for land registration in the state starting from January 2014. As per this directive, for land-related transactions, not only the buyers and sellers but also the witnesses will have to present their Aadhaar number as the proof of identity. It is hoped that Aadhaar card-based land transactions will bring in greater transparency in the sale/purchase of land and prevent registering of the same land more than once.

The results of the pilot initiatives carried out in Jharkhand, starting at the end of 2011 through 2013, have been mixed. Older people and people with restricted mobility have found the initiative especially empowering as it does away with their need to negotiate long distances and banks' bureaucracy or depend on someone else to withdraw their entitlements. Similar empowerment was also reported by women as the Aadhaar-based payment system enabled them to claim their entitlements and even maintain small savings in their own bank accounts. These small savings were to be used for emergencies, which they would earlier hide at home due to the fear of those being taken away by force by their husbands. Alcoholism and domestic violence (often over the issue of control of cash) were reported to be common problems in the villages.

However, in this early stage of experimentation and implementation, some problems emerged. One such problem has been the challenge of ensuring basic infrastructure needed for Aadhaar enrolment and authentication, i.e. power and connectivity, especially in remote, forest areas. If left unaddressed, this problem could result in the residents having to travel to the nearest urban hubs with greater connectivity to claim their entitlement, thus placing them in the pre-Aadhaar situation of having to travel to the nearest bank branches.

The delivery of Aadhaar cards has been one of the most discussed weaknesses of the UID project, both in Jharkhand as well as in other parts of the country. Numerous delays have been reported in the delivery of Aadhaar cards along with instances of cards not being delivered at all. However, the UIDAI has recognised this problem and has started setting up the facility of printing the Aadhaar number using e-Aadhaar at all enrolment centres in order to do away with the dependence on the actual reception of the physical card, and to reduce the time gap between enrolment and the use of Aadhaar to access UID-linked services (Narayan, 2013).

Another problem reported was that of erased or unclear fingerprints especially among rural farm workers and indigenous women and men, which resulted in requiring authentication for the delivery of services. Some cases of authentication problems for MGNREGA and pension payments have been reported from villages in Ranchi, Ramgarh Saraikela-Kharsawan districts.

Aadhaar Enrolment Status in the Field

At the time of the fieldwork (October 2012), the number of residents who have enrolled for Aadhaar in Jharkhand has reached 17,259,568. Of these, approximately 48.4 per cent are women and 51.6 per cent are men. Even though the UIDAI has made a provision for registering transgenders as an independent gender identity group, no enrolment under this category was reflected in the UID data of the state. In terms of distribution by age groups, at 32.3 per cent, the 16–30 age group remains the largest contributor to the overall state registration figures.

As for the geographical distribution of Aadhaar enrolment within the state, Ranchi at 1,949,000 Aadhaars has maintained its lead over other districts since the beginning of UID implementation in the state in 2011. Other districts that have picked up pace in terms of absolute numbers of Aadhaar generated are Dhanbad, Giridih, Bokaro and Hazaribagh.

Fieldwork Sites

Fieldwork was conducted in Jharkhand in October 2012. The fieldwork was organised and carried out jointly with Ranchi-based independent researchers. While constituting the field team, care was taken to include both women and men from the local communities to ensure greater ease of participation as well as to minimise the interference of linguistic and cultural differences with the interpretation of field outcomes. Three districts and seven villages were visited and a total of eight key informant interviews (with a *panchayat* member, an NGO worker or any other knowledgeable person in the village) and 13 Focus Group Discussions (FGDs) were conducted. The discussions conducted were of three kinds: FGDs with only women participants (eight), FGDs with only male participants (three) and combined FGDs with both women and men participants (two).

The districts and villages were selected on the basis of the level of Aadhaar enrolments and the level of introduction of different Aadhaar-enabled services; including special cases such as Dohakatu Panchayat in Ramgarh district, which had received national recognition for its implementation of Aadhaar-based payments in MGNREGA, pensions and student stipends.

The districts for the field visits were Ranchi, Saraikela-Kharsawan and Ramgarh, all of which had been selected by the UIDAI for the Aadhaar-enabled payments project. The villages were: Puriyo (Ranchi), Malmandu (Ranchi), Chitrakota (Ranchi), Nagda (Ranchi), Dohakatu (Ramgarh), Gangudih (Saraikela-Kharsawan), and Jojahatu (Saraikela-

Kharsawan). The average number of participants per village was 61, with an average participation of 33 in each FDG. The total population reached was 430 of which 76 per cent were women and 24 per cent were men.

The questions raised in the FGDs sought to explore the socio-economic situation of the village, the traditional gender identity structures in the region, the existing patriarchal relations, the process of Aadhaar implementation, and whether the new UID scheme was generating an impact on the traditional patriarchal relations and identity structures in these places.

Compared to Andhra Pradesh, the reach of Aadhaar cards was found to be limited in Jharkhand. The approach to the FGDs was slightly altered to adapt to this situation and emphasis was shifted from observation of actual impact to the perception of women and men regarding Aadhaar's potential impact on their well-being in general, and on patriarchal relations in particular.

Aadhaar in the Context of Gender Relations

In all the villages visited, patriarchal structures were observed to be strongly embedded. This could be observed in how women and men conducted themselves during the FGDs. In all the FGDs where both women and men were present, the women would sit on the floor leaving the chairs for the men. It was also observed that in this situation, the women were much less vocal as compared to the only-women FGDs where most women would participate quite actively. However, even in women-specific FGDs, the women were initially hesitant to discuss certain topics such as intra-household relations. However, once they did start discussing the topic, it was observed that these were deep rooted patriarchal relations, which, in many cases, the women justified as 'normal'.

During the field visits in Jharkhand, many positive changes were reported in the last 10 years since the creation of the state. There have been improvements in access to basic facilities such as water, electricity, roads, better yield rice, and greater availability of food. The development has allowed the people of Jharkhand to harbour greater aspirations. However, employment prospects within and around the villages have remained very limited. There had been some talk of mineral deposits in the area and about how it could change the economic scenario.

In several villages included in our study, all children, both girls and boys, were reported to be attending primary school. The drop-out rate of 4 to 5 per cent was reported at the secondary school level, mainly in boys. Announcements, newspaper and television were the main news media in the villages. The main activities for women were reported to be housework, agriculture, employment in MGNREGA (wells, ponds and road building) while the men were engaged either in agriculture or in wage labour outside the village. The crops commonly grown were rice, lentils and vegetables.

Figure 5.1

Focus Group Discussion with Women in Chitrakota Village, Ranchi District

Source: Amber Minz, Ranchi.

Persisting gendered taboos for women include climbing thatched rooftops and touching the plough. They did not break either of these rules for fear of societal punishment, which they believe would imply their ears being cut off. However, some changes could be observed. For example, women could climb the roofs of the modern *pucca* houses. Earlier they could not take out rice or paddy from the storage bin without their husband's permission; however, now they can. *Dayan Bissai* (witch-hunting) was also reported to have decreased significantly. Now women also go to the market to buy and sell minor forest produce and usually hand over the cash to their husband if he is considered of good behaviour. In case the husband is an alcoholic, they would hide the cash from him. Some reduction in domestic violence was also reported in the last 10 years. A significant increase in women's education was also observed during this period. Men help at home when women work or when they are sick.

It was reported that women had land use rights but no control or ownership rights of the land as the *pattas* (title deeds) were in the names of the men of the household. The *patwaris* were almost always men. However, now some women are being trained for the job. Earlier, there used to be some land in women's names. The women recognise the fact that having some land in their names could result in positive changes in their lives. Traditionally, there was no land in women's names. But now, it is reported that there is an increasing trend of buying land in the woman's name to prevent it from falling into the hands of her husband's brother or other male relative. This is more so in cases where an *adivasi* woman is married to a non-*adivasi* man. Further, there is a positive trend of increasing education for girls.

Regarding the increasing participation of women in economic activities outside the house, women felt that it was normal and not problematic. However, some men said that it was their responsibility to take care of the woman and so they didn't like it if the woman earned more than them. However, they said that they liked it if the women were known outside the house due to a government job or such activities.

It was reported that women who are more economically/socially active are now addressed by their own names. However, their children continue to be called by the father's name. Women now increasingly go out of the village to work and to study. However, while men's going out is seen as normal, women who go out are often viewed with suspicion.

Some of the social programmes for women and girls in Chitrakota include the Mukhyamantri Ladli Laxmi Yojana and Mukhyamantri Kanyadaan Yojana. A Christian NGO and a microcredit trust also function in the village. However, nobody in the village received the disability pension. Some women were aware of the existence of a Mahilakosh (Woman's Fund), and were keen to obtain more information on this scheme. Attempts have been made by women in Chitrakota village to organise Women's Self Help Groups (SHGs) and access the funds earmarked for such SHGs. Women were largely distrustful of the correct use of cash by men. Any savings in cash (reported to be extremely limited) was hidden by the women to prevent it from being spent on alcohol.

Notwithstanding, women in Puriyo village (close to Ranchi city and relatively developed economically) were quite vocal about the widespread problem of alcoholism among the men. Alcoholism caused arguments related to money and was cited as the main cause of domestic violence. The incidence of women having to work to run the household while the men would drink and not go to work was reported to be quite high. A social worker active in the village confirmed the prevalence of this problem, and expressed the need for women to raise the issue in public and come together in solidarity to look for solutions for continuing or increased male violence against women.

The research team was informed that various *mahila mandals* (rural women's organisations) had been organised in Puriyo. One of these (Deepa mahila mandal) was functioning extremely well and its members had jointly purchased a piece of land. However, none of the *mahila mandals* of the village had actively participated in the enrolment or awareness process of Aadhaar. In this village, the information about Aadhaar enrolment was given through a *hakua* (village announcement).

Sixteen *mahila mandals* were reported to be functioning in the Malmandu village; of these, 11 were registered and 9 had received seed capital of ₹ 20,000 for starting the group. A project for women's education (till class five) was also reportedly underway. In Malmandu, women could freely use land for agriculture and other purposes but they didn't have any ownership or management rights, and they could not take decisions regarding what to grow or the scale of the produce.

In the village of Jojohatu in Kuchai block of Saraikela-Kharsawan district, many residents, both women and men, were reported to be working in MGNREGS. The MGNREGS payment was made in the bank and the workers had passbooks for withdrawing money. Women usually received less days of work (50) than men (100). Sometimes, they had to pay money to get an MGNREGS job. It was reported that those working in MGNREGS received their wages in cash from the contractor or the mate who withdrew it for them from the post office. In many FGDs, people complained of late/non-/insufficient MGNREGS payments.

During the FGDs, women and men discussed the problem of market intervention in their livelihood, that their earthen wares were no longer in demand as a result of new metal wares in the market. As one man said: "Aluminium has eaten away our livelihood." They were also worried about the increasing use of hybrid seeds and its potential negative impact on the local ecosystem and, eventually, on the economy and society. The solution proposed was agro-processing schemes for farmers and other livelihood schemes from the government.

Gangudih village in the Chandil block of district Saraikela-Kharswan was selected in order to cover some areas that were further from the state capital Ranchi. It has around 350 households and can be reached by a dirt road. The village has no health centre or community centre, but almost all households have an electricity connection. However, the electricity supply is a problem as the voltage is very low and the supply best functions at night after bed time. Chief income generating activities in Gangudih include agriculture, construction work, working in factories and washing gold in the river. Most people own 2–3 *bighas* of land. The land title is in the name of the male members (usually the oldest male member) of the household.

Women worked outside the house for the additional income and men helped in household work, if the woman was sick. Woman in government jobs were known by their own names in the public sphere. However, their decision-making power at home did not change much as a result of their job in the public sphere. Women could not independently take the decision to spend any extra cash, while men could take such decisions. Goods of daily necessity were usually bought by men but sometimes women bought them from a nearby shop. Gendered taboos against the women's use of agricultural equipment such as ploughs have been weakening. Now women can use agricultural tools and equipment but they can't use them to hunt animals and/or to plough fields. The women can use tools to cut wood and to dig. Now women can also help themselves to the rice from the storage bin for household use; however, in case cash is needed, they cannot decide to take out the rice for selling.

Figure 5.2

Focus Group Discussion with Men in Gangudih Village, Saraikela Kharsawan District

Source: Birsa, Ranchi.

Aadhaar Awareness and Wage Payments

The *upmukhiya* of Puriyo *panchayat* (Ranchi district) informed the team that in Ratu block, the UIDAI project was being conducted in three *panchayats*—Puriyo, Taro and Tigra. Most of the FGD participants in Puriyo knew about the Aadhaar card, and a majority of those present had enrolled for UID and received the card. In their experience, the enrolment process had been fairly simple but several cases of problems in registration due to erased finger-lines had been reported.

Aadhaar enrolment in Malmandu (a pilot village for Aadaar-based MGNREGS payments) took place in 2010. It lasted for four to five days. People living and working in Ranchi also came to the village to get enrolled. In the initial camp, in some cases, the Aadhaar officers couldn't record the fingerprints due to erased finger-lines or the iris scan because of cataract. Many residents reported not receiving the card even though they had enrolled several months ago. They didn't know who to contact for grievance readressal. They were also not clear about the order in which the card was being sent as often those who had enrolled with them had already received it. The post office was blamed for its tardiness and inefficiency. With some residents of nearby villages receiving their cards, there was a feeling among Malmandu's residents that their cards may have been delivered to the other villages. All this created anxiety and lack of clarity as to whether the cards that had not arrived were merely delayed or lost. What was needed was the systematic monitoring of actual and correct delivery of the Aadhaar card to see how many of those who have enrolled had not received the card within a specific time limit.

During the FGDs, in Malmandu, an additional problem came to light. One of the participants presented a card that was photocopied and that had someone else's photograph. This practice of photocopying others' cards and changing the name was also reported in another village. It raises some questions regarding the causes behind some of the fingerprints failing to match in the MGNREGS payment scheme (discussed below), and whether some of the failures could be simply due to incorrect numbers or cards presented at the payment site.

A camp for the Aadhaar-linked scheme of MGNREGS payments in Puriyo was held on 2 October 2012. However, the team was told that many payments were not made because the finger-lines did not match. Around 20 to 25 women and men tried the authentication in which only around 10 people were successfully paid. One of the women whose fingerprints did not match during this exercise was present in the FGD; however, she did receive her Aadhaar-based MGNREGS wages from the bank's branch in Ratu. There were others who had successfully received their MGNREGS wages linked with Aadhaar card identification.

The FGD participants pointed out that they had not been informed clearly of the benefits of the Aadhaar card and that many of them had enrolled only out of curiosity and expectation of some future benefits. There were also complaints that banks, schools(at the time of admission) and scholarships did not accept the Aadhaar card and instead still asked for the Below Poverty Line (BPL) card.

Notwithstanding the implementation bottlenecks reported, the perception regarding the potential usefulness of UID was largely positive. If implemented well, Aadhaar could be useful for opening bank accounts, buying SIM cards, travelling by rail, identifying fakes and receiving social entitlements at the doorstep. Similarly, the feature of the micro-ATM machine, whereby the machine gave voice instructions and account information, was appreciated, especially by those residents who could not read or write. The *upmukhiya*, visibly excited by this feature, told us, "The machine is also talking."

The Aadhaar enrolment camp for Chitrakota village (Ratu block) was set up at Pali panchayat. All the enrolment officers were reported to be males. There were long lines for enrolment. Children above four years were enrolled. People from as far as Ranchi, Patna, Delhi, Kolkata, Goa, etc., came to get enrolled for the Aadhaar number. However, many people in the village either could not or did not enrol due to lack of clarity on the utility of Aadhaar. Around 50 per cent of the FGD participants who had enrolled had reportedly not received the card. Some cases of problems in enrolment due to rough fingers were reported. Some names had appeared incorrectly in the final cards received.

In Chitrakota, the villagers had very limited information regarding the nature and benefits of the Aadhaar card. However, some residents had seen the high enrolment levels and the rolling out of the Aadhaar-linked payment scheme in the neighbouring villages of the Puriyo panchayat and were now keen to know more about this new form of identification. Those residents who had already received the card seemed excited about having it and were hopeful about its future utility and benefits. Some of the women reported that they were asked by the bank to bring the Aadhaar card as an identity document for opening the account. They also found it useful for individual identification in case they got lost as it had their address on it. Other possible uses cited were for children's school admission and for buying SIM cards.

Unlike the other villages visited, a smart card system was being introduced in Nagra village of Mandar Block of Ranchi district. There is an Allahabad Bank mini branch in the Panchayat Bhavan of Nagra, in operation for about a year. In early 2012, they had started the smart card scheme at zero cost and with the use of customers' thumbprints. With this card and with the help of a portable biometric authentication machine, the village residents were able to conduct bank transactions such as opening an account, and withdrawing and depositing money. The business correspondent of this bank informed us that this scheme was launched before Aadhaar and was not yet linked to Aadhaar.

Unlike in the other villages, no specific advantages of the Aadhaar card were perceived by the FGD participants in the Nagra village. The villagers felt that all that they would do with the Aadhaar card they already did with the voter ID card. In the discussion on the traditional household-based identification (ration cards), the general feeling was that as long as the woman's name was on the ration card, it was a good enough identification and there wasn't much need for individual identification.

A camp had been organised for Aadhaar enrolment in the local school and it was easy to enrol. Most of the FGD participants knew about Aadhaar and most of them had also enrolled for Aadhaar cards. It was reported that there were a lot of cases of Aadhaar enrolments where the cards had not yet reached. There were hardly any people, women (and men) in the village, who did not have the voter ID card or ration cards. Some women (and men) did not enrol because they didn't realise its importance. However, now they would like to enrol.

The most important use cited for Aadhaar was that of an ID proof. Most participants didn't know of the other possible uses/benefits of Aadhaar but were keen to learn more on its specific benefits. Since many women did not have the card, they said that they found it difficult to discuss its benefits over the earlier IDs. They said that the benefits of Aadhaar cards would only be seen once they started using the card.

In Jojohatu village, information on the Aadhaar enrolment camp was received from the *panchayat*. The residents had hardly any information on Aadhaar and its purpose. Most people (both women and men) enrolled because they were told to. Almost all the FGD participants reported having been enrolled. Out of 30 participants, around 20 had received their cards. It was reported that even those in the village who had not enrolled now wished to enrol.

The information of the final cards having arrived at the local post office was spread by word of mouth. Ward members got the Aadhaar cards from the post office and distributed them. No significant errors were reported in the cards. The women did not feel any change in their confidence level due to Aadhaar as they didn't know of its uses. They got it made due to possible future uses.

An interesting observation in Jojohatu was that children had not been enrolled. The FGD participants weren't aware that children could also get Aadhaar numbers. Amongst the villages visited, this was the only one where the residents weren't aware of children's enrolment. In other villages, children as young as three years old had enrolled in some cases.

Dohakatu panchayat in Ramgarh district was selected for a field visit because, according to an article in the *Times of India* (10 February 2012), Dohakatu panchayat was the first in the country to successfully receive UID-based online payment for various social schemes. The Ramgarh District Magistrate was awarded by the Government of India for exemplary implementation of Aadhaar-enabled services in the district. The visit to Dohakatu confirmed these reports as the researchers could meet in person and talk to some of those who had received payments with their new Aadhaar numbers; among them, one pension receiver, Buddho Devi, was reported highly in the press. Most of the individuals (women and men) present for the FGD had Aadhaar cards and some of them had successfully received payments through the card.

Dohakatu had a very active woman *mukhiya*. She shared some stories about how she had seen people using (photocopied) Aadhaar cards in the other *panchayats*. She also shared that she along with some of those who had received Aadhaar-enabled payments had been invited to other *panchayats* and districts to talk about their experience. In Dohakatu, there was quite a lot of excitement regarding the Aadhaar project and their district being chosen for the national Aadhaar award.

The level of familiarity with Aadhaar there was very high. Around 90 per cent of the village population (both men and women) had Aadhaar cards and they were also familiar with its uses. In this *panchayat*, children above three years were issued Aadhaar numbers. Payments had been made through the Bank of India at the *panchayat* level to MGNREGS workers.

Notwithstanding the wide publicity given to the Aadhaar enrolment at the time of writing this study, we observed the low level of Aadhaar reach during the field work in the state. However, the FGDs, especially with women, did bring out the clear relationship that the women perceived between their economic autonomy and their overall empowerment within the household and outside. In this sense, most women perceived Aadhaar as an initiative that would contribute to their empowerment and to the shifting of decision-making in their favour, mainly by facilitating women's rights to hold bank accounts and possession of land as part of a general increase in their entitlements. It was also interesting to observe that even with an incomplete knowledge of the potential benefits of Aadhaar, most of the women participants were keen to enrol for the Aadhaar number and possess their own Aadhaar cards.

The limited consciousness that was observed in women with respect to Aadhaar as a first individual 'purpose neutral' identity was due in part to the lack of specific women oriented communication and information campaign by the programme. Such campaigns could help achieve the specific potential that the UID programme holds for women's empowerment and positive changes in the state's patriarchal structures. They could also go a long way in shaping women's perception regarding Aadhaar and constitute the difference between women considering Aadhaar as yet another identification document or their viewing it as a unique individual identity that they feel proud to have.

6

Aadhaar Identity and Access to Public Services

The developmental impact of Aadhaar as a biometric identity depends largely on the political and technological context in which it is used. An identity-driven approach to development furthers inclusion, facilitates access to services and strengthens public administration. The Aadhaar project has two utilities for the poor people: (i) expansion of banking services to prior unreached people protecting themselves from financial risks and (ii) optimisation of government programmes for inclusive growth (Planning Commission, 2012). The excluded groups like women, migrants, homeless, destitute, domestic workers, prisoners, aged residents, widows, senior citizens and other vulnerable groups get an identity through Aadhaar by which they can assert their rights as individuals and also access public benefits. Though women's identity is part and parcel of the UIDAI project, the conscious gender dimension was not built into the project. Women's identity can have spin-off gender effects, especially in situations where women's social mobilisation has been in place. Then it becomes important to examine the pathways by which women's identity can lead to women's autonomy and agency and thereby empowerment. It has also been observed from earlier studies that robust identification has increased the risk of exclusion unless effective communication has been set up (Gelb and Clark, 2013).

This applies very much to the remote, rural and indigenous context in the 100 per cent covered district of East Godavari and also several districts of Jharkhand. Because of weak internet connectivity and frequent power outages, the Aadhaar-enabled payment system (AEPS) had limited implementation.

It is correctly argued by Rao that inclusion is a result of the systematic engagement of specific actors, "who mediate a relationship between marginalised citizens and state institutions" (2013: 72). Technological innovations do not act on their own, but through persons, embedded in various types of social, economic and political relations. What a particular technology may enable is a change in the ordering of these relations. The reordering of these relations, however, still needs to be brought about; it is neither automatic nor foreordained. But certain technologies have possibilities that other technologies do not. The traditional documents (ration cards, etc.) have certain possibilities. It could require an element of patronage and/or corruption to acquire enlistment as below poverty line (BPL). This enlistment is subject to being rejected, for some reason or the other. Of course, it is not the ration card that is the source of this restriction; rather, it is the requirement to be certified by someone in power and authority to decide who is eligible on economic grounds. On the other hand, Aadhaar, though it also filters through persons who mediate a relationship between marginalised persons and state institutions, does not have the factor of being rejected—on economic or any other grounds, other than that of already being listed. In fact, it is the latter inclusivity that has led to the political right to attack the Aadhaar Unique Identity (UID) since it does not distinguish between legitimate residents of the country and 'illegal' migrants.

Any other universal document, without a necessarily biometric technology, could do as well in universalising identity. But Aadhaar has the advantage in allowing various agencies, including non-governmental organisations (NGOs) working with the homeless and excluded people, in being mediators in this process. Unlike in the case of the ration card, or for that matter, the election card, it is not the local government officials who can mediate for a person. The multiplicity of such agencies who can mediate works to allow even the urban homeless to secure an Aadhaar identity.

As Rao (2013: 73) points out, the homeless "...remained invisible to the welfare state while being hyper-visible to the police." In the normal course of pre-Aadhaar identification, they would have continued to remain invisible to the welfare state as there would have been no local government authority to vouch for or mediate for them.

The role of such social organisations could possibly account for the reported high level of inclusion in Andhra Pradesh. The vast spread of self-help groups (SHGs) would enable such a high level of inclusion. It is right to say that Aadhaar does not function in a social vacuum. Nor is its inclusionary potential merely a matter of technology. But what is important is that the broad-based process of allowing social mediators to support Aadhaar inclusion could give a more inclusionary outcome than a merely local government-mediated process. This points to a hypothesis: would Aadhaar be more inclusionary in Andhra Pradesh, with its high level of SHG organisation, as compared to Jharkhand where there is much less of such social organisation?

The importance of the Aadhaar card is clearly stated by one of Rao's respondents, who replied to the question "How does that [identity card] help"? with, "The police won't harass us" (Rao, 2013: 76). This statement is important in pointing to the importance of authorised identification when dealing with the state. This is a process of formalisation which gives certain rights; crucially that of not being harassed by the police. Informal methods of dealing with the police put the homeless in a weak position, while Aadhaar is expected to strengthen them in their dealing with police harassment.

The above example is that of persons of unspecified gender. But one can imagine what it would be like for homeless women, who would very likely have to pay with implicit and forced sexual favours to those who could harass them.

Importantly, Aadhaar provides the foundational identity that can be used for social security programmes. In addition, however, Aadhaar can also be used for other economic and social purposes. Aadhaar itself can be used as the basic identification for opening a bank account. With only 25 per cent of Indians now having bank accounts, Aadhaar could increase financial inclusiveness. At present, monetisation of the economy is being extended by the Direct Benefits Transfer (DBT) scheme operated through what are called 'micro-ATMs'. This is a manner of combining Aadhaar-based identified persons, through point of sale instruments, with cash provided by a bank agent who is the one who draws the cash from an ATM. This is a step in monetisation of the economy. But it is still not financial inclusion, which would require the ability to access savings and credit systems, either through an SHG non-banking financial service or directly from a bank. Aadhaar, by providing a foundational identity to a person, can promote the financial inclusion of the 75 per cent who are as yet unbanked. In financial inclusivity, the individual identity of Aadhaar would in particular benefit women, who are otherwise left behind in such schemes directed towards the heads of the household (mostly males).

Figure 6.1

A Micro ATM in Operation in Rural Andhra Pradesh

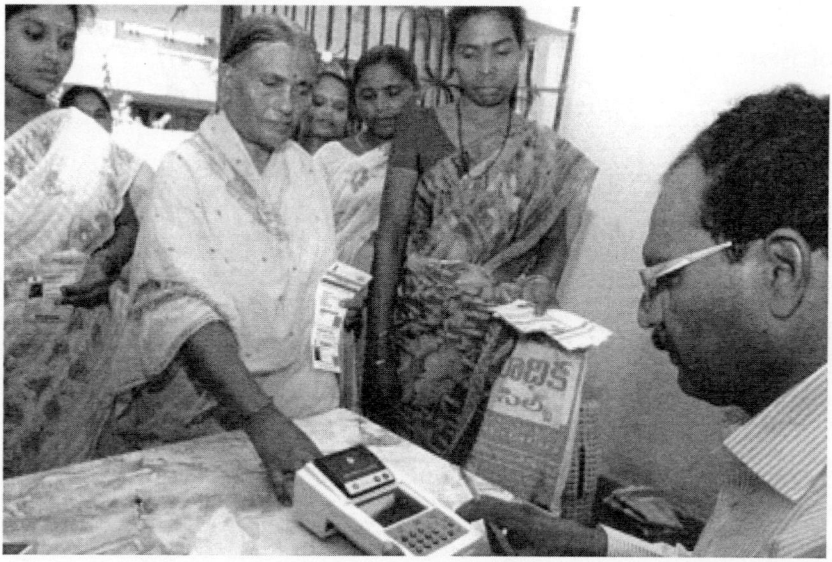

In India, one important obstacle that makes it difficult for certain segments of the population from accessing banking and other financial services, thus excluding them from the mainstream financial system, is their lack of acceptable individual identification and the almost impossibility to fulfill the KYC (know your customer) norms. From the perspective of the banking service providers, some of the obstacles that perpetuate this financial exclusion are the high last mile cost for account opening and managing; technological limitations for effectively opening and managing these accounts; and the low revenue potential of these customers.

At a very basic level, holding a unique formal identity such as Aadhaar will help facilitate the access to financial services to those who have been excluded so far from such services due to the mere fact of not holding valid identity documents. However for true financial inclusion to take place, many other mechanisms need to be put in place.

In this sense, in conjunction with the Aadhaar programme, steps are being taken to proactively link Aadhaar to various facets of financial services to ensure greater financial inclusion through Aadhaar. Some of the steps in this regard are: making Aadhaar an acceptable KYC, thus making it easier for potential customers to open accounts, as well as reducing the customer acquisition costs for the banks; and leveraging the UID enrolment platform and efforts for parallel accounts opening process, thus reducing costs and efforts both for clients as well as for banks. Currently, in most of rural and isolated areas in India, people have limited access to financial services. There are not many banks operating in rural and indigenous areas; the service delivery network is very limited. UIDAI's plan to issue Aadhaar to 60 crore residents over a four-year period offers a unique opportunity in this regard to break this vicious circle of financial exclusion and make it a virtuous circle of inclusion.

Financial Inclusion

In a discussion paper on financial inclusion (Task Force, 2011), UIDAI highlighted some other advantages of the biometric Aadhaar individual identity: facilitation of government payment disbursal directly to individuals through their Aadhaar-enabled bank accounts; lower transaction cost for banks (through elimination of smart cards) and increased security for customers (doing away with the risks of the smart cards being stolen or misused by others, a concern especially important in the case of women customers) resulting from online Aadhaar authentication. Adoption of Aadhaar online authentication would also increase the number of service points for the banks and their customers as this solution will be interoperable; thus customers of one bank will also be able to access the service points of another bank as both banks will be using the same online authentication system. Apart from providing the customers with greater choice and reducing their dependence on a single service provider, this will also lead to optimisation of resources across banks and result in cost-effective mechanisms.

Regarding some more complex financial services, introduction of Aadhaar in a bank's database will allow the bank to uniquely identify its customers across various product offerings and form a holistic view for portfolio management. This will benefit banks by allowing them to form a much more informed view on their existing customer profiles and in offering new products/services to them. Moreover, adoption of Aadhaar in the bank databases will enable easy merger of customer data across banks, and thus provide a tremendous impetus to the usage of Credit Bureaus in the country and enable banks to make informed decisions in offering new products/services to customers by leveraging the customer's credit history not only for their bank's products, but also for products/services availed from other banks.

Even though the inclusion into the financial system and in the mainstream economy of the hereto excluded segments of the population is in itself a positive development, both for the individuals as well as the economy as a whole, care should be taken to ensure that new kinds of exclusions and risks or infringement of personal rights do not take place in the process. Both more efficient account opening as well as more effective management of accounts and customers' portfolios are based on the online nature of the system allowing for easier sharing of customers' data among UIDAI (public database) and different service providers (private data base).

It is of vital importance that any such measures are preceded by a strong and suitable legal system to prevent the infringement of personal privacy and accompanied by close monitoring to ensure that the customers' consent for opening accounts, for present or future data sharing, is obtained only after apprising the individuals concerned of the risks involved in such data sharing. This is of special significance as the target population for financial inclusion is precisely comprised of segments that are more vulnerable (rural and indigenous women) to risks due to lower levels of literacy, and limited exposure to complex financial services and information. However, care should be taken to see that Aadhaar enrolment is voluntary and does not turn involuntary in case of parallel processes for banking or for other financial services.

Once there is a foundational identity system in place, many other uses can be built on that system. Programmes would have to be developed for various uses.

Access to Public Services

Aadhaar could help make public service and entitlement delivery more efficient, transparent and inclusive even without making any radical changes in the system. Public education, health system, and social entitlement systems such as MGNREGA, public distribution system (PDS) and LPG subsidies are some of the examples.

As the UIDAI task force discussion paper (Task Force, 2011) points out, Aadhaar could play an important role in the education sector, in the delivery of books and stationery to schools and students based on the biometric authentication to ensure that these entitlements actually reach those who they are meant for, and that any fraud in claiming the entitlements by intermediaries can be reduced and more easily tracked. Teachers´ absenteeism is a major problem in India´s education system. UID based attendance tracking could help reduce this problem. Similarly, over reporting of registration and students' attendance is rampant; which apart from wastage of limited resources, makes it difficult to collect credible statistics, understand the underlying problems and to implement appropriate solutions. Thus using UID to track students' attendance would help solve these problems, as well as allow better planning and public resources management. Lastly, the portability of Aadhaar (and ideally, Aadhaar linked school records) would be an important step forward for migration between schools and will be of special help to children belonging to traditionally migrant communities.

In the context of the public health system of a country as vast and complex as India, where much of the population remains unidentified, it is very difficult to obtain a clear understanding of the target population and their needs to be addressed via the rural and the urban health systems. New-born children cannot be easily tracked, so vaccination cannot be ensured. Aadhaar enrolment number would help the government define a more informed national health strategy, and provide infrastructure and resources according to objective needs assessment (Hamza and Narain, 2013). Apart from better overall monitoring and planning at national and local levels, Aadhaar could also play an important role in controlling absenteeism among the medical staff, enhancing the efficiency of public health subsidies and incentive schemes such as the Janani Suraksha Yojana (JSY), checking on the immunisation and health status of babies as well as for other medical uses such as keeping track of the medicine intake of tuberculosis patients.

MGNREGS Payments

Since its introduction, the MGNREGA has played an important role in the rural economies of the country both at the household as well as the community levels. A minimum number of days of work per year is ensured to each household for creating public works and other productive infrastructure. However, the implementation of the programme has been assailed by a number of problems; one of the important ones being that of corruption (manifested in various ways), but whose end result is that only a small percentage of money for wage payments that flows out of the exchequer actually reaches the workers. One way this is achieved is by over reporting attendance and by generating pay rolls of ghost workers. Aadhaar-enabled attendance at the point of work would help control over-reporting of workers and make it difficult to create muster rolls made up of ghost workers.

Similarly, the point of work attendance could be matched against the Aadhaar number of the worker to whom the wages are being paid to ensure that they are the same. The Aadhaar number system could also help in better monitoring of the scheme and help collect sex-disaggregated data on the level of women´s participation in MGNREGA payment, the kind of work done by them, as well as the wages being paid to them. This information could be a valuable input for future policy and programme design. As discussed earlier, payment of wages to workers in their Aadhaar-enabled bank accounts (accessible through a network of BCs) could reduce delays in the payments and reduce the dependence of workers on intermediaries for their payments. This phenomenon of breaking the workers' dependence on intermediaries could be even more important for women who are more vulnerable than men (due to their socio-cultural standing, literacy levels etc.) in such situations.

India´s PDS is highly inefficient with high level of corruption and leakages resulting in the exclusion of a big number of citizens from their actual entitlement (generally segments of the population who need it the most) and a large number of intermediaries who benefit from the leakages in the system and from the black market for basic products that results from the diversion of products from their legitimate distribution through the fair price shops (FPS).One possible way of making the system efficient is through a dramatic shift in the nature of the PDS, from food to cash entitlements. Even as this shift is debated, the biometric based UID can be put to use to reduce the current level of leakages. One way is to use biometric authentication of customers at the point of sale to ensure that ration is only withdrawn by those who are entitled to it. UID authentication can be used to plan future allocation to any FPS, based on the people it serves, giving FPS managers strong incentive to properly authenticate their beneficiaries. Another way is to create accountability in the supply side of the system through biometric authentication of the dealers and of other intermediaries, combining it with GPS tracking of the supplies trucks.

Some other uses of Aadhaar that have been discussed or that are being piloted are: reduction in electoral fraud, implementing caps on subsidised LPG, more dynamic monitoring of population level and growth, etc.

Questioning Aadhaar Technology

There are objections to Aadhaar on the ground that it could be used to exclude persons or social groups from receiving benefits. One of the arguments that has been used the most to question the shift to Aadhaar-enabled direct benefit transfers (DBTs) has been the impact it has on the very nature of the social welfare and protection system from a human rights-based system to a more targeted and individualised one. Civil society activists have raised concerns about making social entitlements dependent on possessing an Aadhaar number. Apart from its implications for the individual decision to enrol or not to enrol in a biometric database, it also poses a risk of exclusion from entitlements for those who may remain involuntarily unidentified, for example, due to problems with enrolments in certain remote rural and indigenous are as, indefinite delays in delivery of the numbers, etc.

What Aadhaar can do is deal with exclusion based on non-possession of portable identity. It can help increase the inclusiveness of the banking system. It can help migrant children establish their identity in order to be able to access schools wherever they go. The inclusion of transgender in the UID is reported to be a move forward towards more legality for hitherto invisible transgender people (Aneka, 2011). The UID is seen a useful way to start the push for their identity proof and thereby citizenship rights.

Fears have also been raised about the identity data that would be available to the state for profiling of dissidents. The data with Aadhaar is very minimal; just biometric identity, name, gender and address. This is very basic and nothing like the data currently available with mobile phone companies and banks.

In fact, Aadhaar can be a powerful instrument against identity theft. On the internet, through banking and credit card systems, identities can be stolen. But a person's Aadhaar identity cannot be stolen. Even if the card is lost, the Aadhaar number exists. Even if the number is forgotten, through biometric checking, a person can regain the Aadhaar number. In case of identity theft, Aadhaar can be used to reestablish identity. Of course, this is more a matter for the better-off than the poor. But the fact that Aadhaar cannot be stolen and can be used to restore stolen identities is an important point in its favour.

Given the controversy over Aadhaar, the strategy followed has been that of a demand-driven exercise rather than making it mandatory for all residents to register for UID. Increasingly, incentives have been put in place so that people would find it in their own benefit to enrol for Aadhaar. Most such incentives are related to accessing public services and subsidies.

Some central ministries had raised objections to Aadhaar on the grounds that rural areas with poor connectivity would not be able to use the online Aadhaar system. They argued in favour of smart card-based offline systems. The smart card system can eliminate ghosts or non-existent persons but it cannot detect duplicates. It can verify whether A is A, but cannot show whether she has many smartcards. The Aadhaar system can do both—eliminate ghosts and eliminate duplicates.

The experience of Andhra Pradesh is instructive in this matter. Initially, the government decided to have a smart card based on the PDS. But within a short while, there were millions of fakes. Then a switch was made to the Aadhaar system. With about 60 per cent of the verification completed, over 7 million duplicate ration cards, 255,000 duplicate pensions and 347,000 duplicate housing beneficiaries were detected. All this resulted in a saving that paid for more than the $10 million cost of the backend software (Zelazny, 2012: 33). In Andhra Pradesh, there are reportedly more BPL ration cards than there are households.

Necessary Safeguards

If the technological systems are available, it is safe to assume that various government agencies will try to use them for their own interests. Laws provide a base for resistance to such use, but laws will also need the support of a vigilant civil society.

There is need for safeguards with stronger privacy measures and safety legislations. Safeguards are needed not only in the case of commercial uses but also for governmental uses. Aadhaar can be used by the government to build profiles not only of 'terrorists' but of all dissidents. A religious fundamentalist government may use it for profiling minorities. Citizens will need safeguards against such uses by the government to suppress dissent or victimise minorities. A vibrant civil society will need to formulate laws and other measures to prohibit and check such uses.

It should also be pointed out that the digitisation of information has helped governments and also citizens to use this technology to expose illegal or otherwise dubious actions of governments. For example, Wikileaks or Snowden's revelations about the United States government's digital spying in the whole world are testimony to the increasing power of global citizens to use digitisation to expose government wrongdoings/misuse of power. Of course, here too, such exposure can be for good or bad, and requires vigilance from global citizens.

The use of technology for state surveillance exists not only with regard to national governments but also other governments. Cyber and mobile phone space can be broken into by non-national governments too. The spying by US agencies on various world leaders shows the need to be vigilant against the misuses of technology. The defence against such misuse is not to eschew all such technologies and the benefits they bring. A vigilant civil society will need to work on ways to counter state, non-state and other state surveillance. At this time, the contours of such safeguards may not be visible; but this is something on which work will need to be done.

The European Union already has a series of biometric databases on its citizens. However, it also possesses strong privacy laws to protect its citizens. Technological leapfrogging in India will need to be political and social to have adequate laws and a technologically-adept gender inclusive civil society.

We live in a world that has both a physical and a virtual existence. In India, large numbers are outside that virtual existence. Aadhaar is a major step in extending virtual existence to all, one that will be complemented by the rapidly-growing smart mobile phone to enable most to be actively connected to both physical and virtual worlds. As we grow accustomed to this change, we also learn that the two worlds are not mutually exclusive, and what happens in one has consequences for the other (Schmidt and Cohen, 2013). Such consequences will be extended from a minority to almost all. Learning to negotiate the two worlds will become a requirement for all, women and the poor included.

7

Efficiency: Service Providers and Service Receivers

There are two types of benefits that could accrue with Aadhaar. One is to the state to be able to implement social protection schemes with less cost and more efficiently. The other is to individuals, particularly to the poor and women, to be included in social protection schemes, and to secure other benefits such as access to banking and other formal financial services. We will consider the likely benefits to the state first and then move to inclusion of women and other excluded social groups.

The biggest benefit of biometric and online identification systems is that they can eliminate duplicates (one person with multiple cards) and ghosts (non-existent persons being registered). In Botswana, biometric identification reduced the number of people receiving pensions by 25 per cent. In Nigeria, biometric identification similarly reduced pensioners by 40 per cent (Gelb and Clark, 2012).

As explained by the Union Minister of Rural Development, Jairam Ramesh (*The Hindu*, 2012) that the initiative of direct benefit transfer (DBT) is the real tool against corruption that is likely to ensure that the state does not degenerate into a non-functioning one. Some of the positive effects of DBTs that the Minister of Rural Development outlined are: (i) DBTs through biometrically operated Aadhaar-enabled bank accounts would significantly reduce the problem of duplicates and ghost beneficiaries; (ii) they would enable the benefits to reach the intended people directly cutting down the layer of intermediaries and on time; (iii) a sufficiently developed network of business correspondents (BCs) with micro ATMs would enable the financial service delivery to the rural and the excluded people, ensuring their inclusion in the mainstream economy.

It should be noted that these reductions occurred not by exclusion, but by eliminating duplicates, ghosts and the deceased. Such elimination and the reduction of payments is a benefit to the service providers, to the government agencies, and a saving for the exchequer.

For the individual service receivers, biometric identification is reported to have provided benefits through "payments reaching their intended destinations with little deviation and that the costs to the recipient of realizing the payments were very small" (Gelb and Clark, 2013: 44). Another important benefit is that payments meant for women were paid to them rather than to their husbands or brothers, as has often been the practice in many development schemes. In South Africa, it was noted that a lack of documents was one of the main reasons why so many poor families were not able to claim their benefits (Hanlon *et al.*, 2010).

Aadhaar is of utility to both service receivers (economically poor women and men) and service providers (the various government agencies). Taking the utility to service providers, Aadhaar can be used to detect duplicates and ghost holders. An Aadhaar-based check in Karnataka found that more than one-fourth (2,400,000 out of 7,900,000) of LPG connections were fake (Mehdudia, 2012). Domestic LPG connections, with a cost of ₹ 28 per kg, were being diverted to commercial use, where the supply price was ₹ 80 per kg.

Registering non-existent persons is a way of corruption, whether in the case of MGNREGS workers, LPG or kerosene claimants. Halting or reducing corruption is a saving to the government. The extent of savings due to weeding out of non-existent or duplicate registrations would depend on the extent of such fraudulent claims. From the example above and other such information, the extent of such savings could range from 25 per cent as in case of LPG connections to 10 per cent in case of MGNREGS works (NCAER, 2005).

Aadhaar should be seen as part of the process of technologically streamlining the administrative system. In conjunction with GPS (global positioning system) tracking, it could be used to check diversions and also to keep track of projects. GPS tracking is being used in Chhattisgarh to check the movement of grain and to reduce bulk diversion of public distribution system (PDS) grain into the open market during transit. In Uttar Pradesh, the state government has initiated GPS registration of MGNREGS projects. These were introduced to eliminate the possibility of double payment for the same work. It can also be used to keep track of progress in work and payments.

The most important use of Aadhaar is to reduce the costs of transfer of funds in various entitlement schemes. This requires a combination of the online recognition system with a basic banking service that is being developed with handheld instruments. The Aadhaar Payments Bridge (APB) and the Aadhaar-enabled payments system (AEPS) are some of the examples of the use of Aadhaar by commercial organisations to facilitate transactions. The AEPS and APB are in the process of being used not just by government departments, but also by commercial organisations such as ICICI Bank and Visa.

For use in PDS transactions, online recognition is combined with point-of-sale (POS) instruments. This is reported to have reduced the cost of PDS operations by 10 per cent in Gujarat and by 15 per cent in Andhra Pradesh (Abraham, 2012). As mobile scanning systems are developed, one can expect a further reduction in cost as a result of increased use of Aadhaar. An International Monetary Fund (IMF) report estimated that the savings of combining direct cash transfer with Aadhaar could be up to 0.5 per cent of the gross domestic product (GDP) (IMF, 2013).

Cash Transfers/DBTs and Subsidies

Using Aadhaar for cash-to-cash transactions is relatively simple. Old age pensions or school stipends can be transferred through Aadhaar to the personal accounts of the persons concerned. But changing from kind to cash systems will be more difficult and would need to be carried out in a step-by-step manner, rather than as a 'big bang' change. The step-by-step method indeed is how the government is going about implementing the Aadhaar scheme.

There are some important problems that need to be dealt with in the movement from distributing materials in kind (i.e., subsidised kerosene, LPG or grain) to cash transfers. One is that transfers should be both assured and timely. In the absence of timely payments, it would not be possible for intended receivers to make their budgets. As the example of non-timely payments for kerosene subsidies shows, intended recipients may be unable to use the payments. This is a problem that could be resolved with an improvement in management systems (Bhatti and Khanna, 2012).

A more important issue here is that of maintaining the real value of subsidies. The cash transfers would have to be linked to the market prices, so that the amounts that can be purchased correspond to the intended subsidy. Without such a price link, the real value of cash subsidies would be eroded over time. This did occur in Sri Lanka and it eroded the real value of cash subsidies.

A pilot study carried out by SEWA Bharat (2012) for the Delhi government brings out interesting results. The study was carried out in 2011 in West Delhi with voluntary target and control groups. The target groups were given PDS benefits in cash instead of in-kind benefits through ration shops. An interesting aspect of the study was that right from the outset, it took into account the potential risks of disempowerment as well as the global evidence that giving benefits to women increases the probability of justice in intra-household distribution as well as focus on basic priority goods such as nutrition, health, etc.

Some of the main findings of this study are: (i) no adverse effect of cash transfers on food security; (ii) positive effect of cash transfers on household nutrition (by providing the household the choice of introducing more nutritious food as per their needs); (iii) no increase in alcohol consumption in households with cash transfers; (iv) increased empowerment of women (reflected by their greater role in household decision-making) as a result of cash transfer into women's bank accounts.

A more recent study by SEWA and UNICEF (2012) conducted in nine villages of Madhya Pradesh noted important benefits from individualised cash transfers. The small cash transfers of ₹ 300 per adult (woman and man) and ₹ 150 per child were given to individuals and not to the household as a unit. Children's entitlement was given to the mother. The study reported a number of well-being impacts: e.g., an increase in children's nutrition, particularly of girls' weight-for-age increases. Women who received not only their share but also that of their children surely had a greater role in the household decision-making than before.

There was no higher incidence of spending on alcohol or tobacco. This finding is important to note, as it shows results against the usual assumption that more cash in the poor household hands leads to greater wastage by men in particular. Such wastage was not observed even in the case of cash in men's hands. Both women and men used these amounts on quality education of their children, with transport and English-based training and schooling. A number of them increased investment (though tiny amounts in own account, small business and acquisition of land for agricultural production. Furthermore, "individualised cash grants gave household members with disabilities greater voice in how money was spent" (SEWA and UNICEF, 2012: 4).

A cash transfer in place of sale at subsidised prices has the advantage of having all transactions carried out at market prices. Establishing a one-price system eliminates the price differential factor leading to diversion of subsidised food and other commodities, from being supplied to, say, BPL households to open market sales. The greater the price differential between subsidised and open market prices, the more the incentive to divert sales. In fact, this profit from illegal diversion is what makes running a PDS store attractive and has created a huge lobby in favour of commodity transfers. Cash transfers would eliminate this diversion, but would need to overcome the political resistance to such a change.

But there is one important problem that cash transfers or DBTs would not resolve—the problem about the exclusion of poor persons and households from the BPL lists. Where entitlements are conditional on being enlisted, then exclusion from the BPL lists is a problem that cannot be solved by Aadhaar or any other such identity system. The exclusion of the poor from beneficiary lists can be resolved by one method—by making the entitlements universal. This, however, would raise the issue of the cost of providing the income support to the non-poor. This, too, can be taken care of by an appropriate system of taxes to recover the amounts transferred to the non-poor. Further, few would question that non-exclusion of the poor is better than inclusion of the non-poor.

In an interview with *The Hindu* (January 2013)Amartya Sen warns against the transition to DBTs without considering short-term transition and cultural shocks, which could negatively affect those in the highest need of and more dependent on public subsidies. Sen also points to the importance of being aware of the possible losers in a transition to cash transfers (children, women) and the need for an in-depth analysis and careful design keeping in mind the transition costs, the potential losers, in order to control such negative effects.

A study for the Asian Development Bank (ADB) estimated that in 2004–05, of about ₹ 20,000 spent on grain subsidy, only about 10 per cent went to the poor. Some 19 per cent went to the non-poor, 43 per cent was diverted and 28 per cent was excess cost due to inefficiency in the government management of logistics. Of their total monthly consumption of 8 or 9 kg, the bottom decile received only 1 kg from the PDS; the rest was bought from the market. This is about 11 to 12.5 per cent of their grain consumption. But if we look at their total monthly consumption, then it was only 2.5 per cent for the bottom decile (Chaudhuri and Somanathan, 2011: 77–80).

If there were an Aadhaar-enabled cash transfer, then the benefits would not just be from the reduction of diversion but also from the increased funds available for transfer, and also from the cost savings compared to the PDS. Suppose that all of the amount spent by the government on PDS subsidy were transferred as cash to all but the top decile, then the bottom decile would get almost three times as much as they get now, about 6 per cent of monthly per capita consumption expenditure. Through the PDS, this would amount to 8 per cent of the monthly expenditure for the bottom decile. With an Aadhaar-enabled DBT, this would go up to as much as 14 per cent of monthly per capita expenditure of the bottom decile.

What Aadhaar can do is to reduce fraudulent use through duplication and ghost registration. In these ways, Aadhaar can increase the efficiency of the administrative system in supplying entitlements, whether in cash or in kind, through targeted delivery. But for a system of entitlements, particularly in cash, to work well, what is needed is assured and timely payments. Aadhaar makes it easier to administer a system of entitlements, and thus reduces costs and increases the efficiency of the entitlements system.

Migration

An increasingly important aspect of contemporary economic development, as it was in the past, is the transfer of populations from areas of surplus labour to areas where the demand for labour is growing; the rural to urban transfer of working people is a key aspect of structural transformation in a labour-surplus economy such as India. In a state like Bihar, migration is a key aspect of day-to-day economic life. More than half of the households surveyed across Bihar by the Institute for Human Development (IHD) had at least one migrant worker, and migrants accounted for one-fourth of the total labour force of the state (Rodgers *et al.*, 2012). The importance of migration to local well-being is seen in that migrants' remittances accounted for more than one-third of consumption as against just three per cent from social protection transfers (Reddy *et al.*, 2012; Nathan and Sharma, 2012).

From the high level of migration, it can be argued that a social protection system must be both universal and portable. But a problem with the current system is that the entitlements are not portable. Subsidised food grain is available only in the village in which one is registered. School subsidies too are available to children only in their own village. This increases the costs of migration.

Aadhaar is the first step in establishing portability. But Aadhaar is only a means of establishing or verifying identity. The next question that needs to be addressed is: what kind of social protection system would better meet the needs of portability; the provision of subsidised goods, such as food grain, or a cash transfer referred to as a DBT in India?

Subsidised food can be provided even in the destination areas. But their supply depends on shopkeepers being able to estimate and ask for the needed food grain. In this situation, even if the right to subsidised food were made portable, ration shop keepers are likely to deny access to migrants on the ground of not having received the requisite supplies. A cash transfer on the other hand would not need such a calibration of supplies. In a reasonably well-functioning market system, supplies could increase in seasons of migration, without any effect on prices. Cash transfers also have the advantage of allowing the household to be flexible in using its resources. In one month the priority might be children's school fees, while it may be medical expenses in another or food in a third. In addition, cash transfers would reduce transportation costs in having to make repeated visits to ration shops. Of course, cash transfers through Aadhaar would require the extension of financial inclusion. In fact, the need for all recipients to have bank accounts would push forward financial inclusion.

To sum up, a portable system of social protection is needed to enable migrant workers to benefit from social protection. Such a portable system requires the foundation of an identity system, such as Aadhaar, and is best conducted through cash transfers rather than direct provision of subsidised commodities.

Costs and Benefits of Aadhaar

In November 2012, the National Institute of Public Finance and Policy (NIPFP) released a cost benefit analysis (CBA) of the Aadhaar project (NIPFP, 2012). The report outlined the major intangible and tangible benefits. The intangible benefits included increases in labour mobility, demand-side empowerment and inclusion. The tangible benefits to governance and economy were stated to be: reduction in leakages and efficiency improvement in implementation of MGNREGS, PDS, education and fertiliser and LPG subsidies. The benefits to economy are likely to be reduction in fraud (due to better and cheaper KYC for all women and men), lowering of transaction costs and gains with efficient management. These benefits were compared to the costs of building and integrating various schemes with Aadhaar, with the assumption that there would be a lag in integrating these schemes with Aadhaar.

The costs of building and integrating various schemes were estimated at a present value of ₹ 371 billion. Estimated over the period of 10 years (from 2010-11 to 2020-21) and taking into account the project´s impact on public finances, its internal rate of return (IRR) in real terms sums up to 52.85 per cent; as future government savings, resulting from a reduction of leakages from major public schemes and subsidies, will compensate the cost of the initiative within the first 10 years. The schemes considered were nine in all—PDS, MGNREGS, fertiliser and LPG subsidies, Mid Day Meal Scheme, Indira Awas Yojana, Janani Suraksha Yojana, Accredited Social Health Activist and the Integrated Child Development Scheme.

The exercise undertaken by NIPFP was a CBA of Aadhaar´s impact on public finances. Social impact of the programme such as greater social inclusion of rural and marginal groups, women's empowerment etc. was not estimated. The question raised by the report was whether the costs of Aadhaar can be easily compensated by future savings in public expenditure. The analysis has been done in absolute terms, as Aadhaar has not been compared to other potential alternatives. The fact that only very limited economic gains have been included in the analysis (leaving out most of the potential social benefits), makes it difficult to compare the result with other social/governance programmes.

The analysis divides the potential benefits arising from Aadhaar into two categories: tangible benefits and intangible benefits. Most of the potential social impacts of the initiatives have been considered intangible benefits, thus excluding any attempt at estimating the social impact of the project.

The tangible benefits are further divided into: (i) tangible benefits for the economy; and (ii) tangible benefits for the government. It then proceeds to assume tangible benefits to the economy to be zero and does not include them in the analysis. Within the tangible benefits for the government, the analysis focuses on the potential public savings derived from the reduction in leakages in 7 major public schemes and subsidies which will be linked to Aadhaar. Some other potential benefits for the government such as gains from increased efficiency or from better programme coordination, etc. are also excluded from the calculations. Following this logic, an IRR of 52.8 per cent was arrived at. What is important to note that Aadhaar can enable a change in the method of transferring benefits, particularly in the case of PDS food grain. The physical distribution of grain involves administrative, storage and transportation costs. Switching to a system of cash transfer, or what is being called DBT, will lead to a saving of these administrative costs. Storage and distribution costs will not be borne by the government, but by the private traders in the process.

There are rather conservative estimates of the extent of losses due to leakages. For instance, in the case of the PDS, it was taken at 12.5 per cent of the total expenditure. In addition, the benefits that were taken into account were very limited, just leakages due to duplicate and ghost identities. This estimate of benefits is on the basis of Aadhaar being used with everything else in these schemes remaining the same, including the physical method of providing the benefits.

This implies that if the project has been found to be easily viable at the current IRR of over 50 per cent, monetisation and inclusion of any additional benefits (such as its mid-long term positive impacts in increasing women's autonomy and agency) will only result in higher IRR i.e. a more positive result (assuming no significant social cost raise from the initiative).

The CBA conducted by NIPFP allows us to analyse the economic viability of Aadhaar but not its effectiveness in reaching its own social goals. More in-depth and complex analysis that would take into consideration the social and governance aspects as well as allow us to compare it with other possible options over which it was chosen, will go a long way towards helping establish Aadhaar as a real 'game changer' in policy effectiveness and financial inclusion.

8

Two Types of Convergence and a Third

Aadhaar itself is only a biometric identification system. It does not contain any information other than personal details (name, parents' and spouse's name), biometrics and address. But other programmes can be linked with Aadhaar. For instance, sales from the public distribution system (PDS) could be based on Aadhaar cards, the way they are now based on smart cards in Andhra Pradesh. Various other programmes like Mahatma Gandhi National Rural Employment Guarantee Act scheme (MGNREGS), Janani Suraksha Yajana (JSY), Integrated Child Development Scheme (ICDS), etc. could all be linked with Aadhaar. Duplicates and ghost payments or transfers could be weeded out from all these systems. This leads to a form of convergence with all these programmes depending on Aadhaar for their payments. A convergence of government programmes through Aadhaar would reduce administrative costs in all these programmes, in addition to providing the obvious benefit of savings through eliminating duplicates and ghosts.

But there can be another form of convergence too. This could be of a commercial or a business type. Banks, insurance companies, microfinance institutions and such other commercial organisations could link their data sets with Aadhaar. In addition, these silos of information (banking, insurance, etc.) could all be linked up or act as bridges between the silos through Aadhaar. Aadhaar by uniquely identifying each person could be used to build up a banking or debt-based profile of an individual. This has been characterised as crafting a "consumer citizen, defined dominantly by debt legibility" as against the supposedly earlier "identity in India that was overwhelmingly concentrated as a political subject involving rights, duties and obligations" (Shukla, 2010: 31).

The literature referred to above deals with two kinds of convergence, those of the political subject and of the consumer citizen. But there is a third convergence, which is of strategic interest for development—that of women as both political subjects and consumer citizens. Women are often not separately brought into such discussions on subjects and citizens. They often do figure as consumers. Commercial organisations are usually more aware of the role of women as consumers than are political and social analysts of the non-feminist variety. Thus, we would like to highlight the issue of convergence with regard to women, too, both as political subjects and as consumer citizens.

The two, political citizen and consumer citizen, do not negate or go against each other. One can be both a political citizen with various rights and obligations, and also a consumer citizen, carrying out various transactions, including acquiring and settling debt. For a long part of our postcolonial history, large sections of the population were not considered to be consumer citizens. Though they definitely were consumers, their consumption was so minimally above subsistence that they were not really considered consumers. The growth of the Indian economy and the spread of a market-based economy have been rapidly changing this scenario. Some amount of discretionary spending, even if it is minimally so for toiletries or intoxicants, is present across the country and even in the lowest consumption groups. These are addressed by what are called 'bottom of the pyramid' production and marketing strategies. Along with this, there is also the expansion of the microcredit system, much more so in south India. This has brought even lower consumption deciles into the formal credit system. They were always part of the credit, but that was of the informal moneylender variety.

In one way or the other, lower consumption deciles have also emerged as 'consumer citizens'. But the process is very uneven. Vast sections, 75 per cent of the population, still do not have access to the formal banking system. Aadhaar seeks to carry forward this market-oriented transformation of the economy by providing a foundational identity that can be used for commercial purposes. For instance, banks have been asked to accept the Aadhaar card as an identity card for opening a 'no frills', zero-balance banking account. Of course, not all banks will agree to open such 'no frills' accounts, and will insist on income details and minimum balances. The compliance with such a government rule may be fitful. But the rule is there and can be the base for pressing for such a facility. Even a sceptical analyst of the unique identity (UID) points out that some homeless in Delhi were able to open such accounts, though the numbers are few and required mediation from non-governmental organisations (NGOs) to be brought about (Rao, 2013: 75).

If the consumer already exists, along with the political citizen, then what is the debate about? There are two points in the debate. The first is whether the state should be a mediator and facilitator of the market (Shukla, 2010: 31). The second is whether there should be a shift from the existing informal processes of economic transactions to a formalised process (Maringanti, 2009: 39).

Being a facilitator of the market is nothing new for the state. Enforcing the rule of law, the law of contracts, building infrastructure—all these and many other measures are undertaken by the state to facilitate markets. Some of these measures, such as enforcing contracts, also mediate between enterprises in the market. These, however, do not exhaust the functions of the state in market-based development.

When markets fail and economic structures do not allow a minimum level of existence, it is then the function of the state to provide a manner of social minimum. The PDS and MGNREGS are state measures to provide a social minimum. There are other measures of income transfer too, such as state-provided old age or widow pensions, free schooling, and so on. These are all part of the redistributive functions of the state.

When the Washington Consensus held sway, there was an emphasis only on the market facilitating functions of the state. Its redistributive functions were ignored in a type of market fundamentalism. Since the onset of the current global economic crisis, however, there has been a struggle to reassert the redistributive functions of the state.

In the context of the debate about Aadhaar, what needs to be reiterated is that the state's market facilitating functions do not exhaust its role in the economy. The state should also play a redistributive function. The demand for the state to play a redistributive function is often placed in terms of the rights of citizens, or the political citizen. But meeting the rights of citizens as political agents is not opposed to the state also playing a facilitating role in the economy. Such a facilitating role of the state is, in fact, critical to promote economic development.

Formalisation of Rights

The other point of the debate is that of formalisation. Aadhaar is a major step in formalisation. The middle and upper classes have had the benefit of formalisation, whether in the credit system or in economic rights. But there are vast numbers in the informal economy who do not receive the benefits of formalisation. The rule that Aadhaar identification should be sufficient for opening a bank account does not mean that financial inclusion will be achieved, but it makes it possible.

The commercial bank-linked self-help group (SHG) system in Andhra Pradesh is also such a measure of financial inclusion, one that took place without Aadhaar. But with increasingly mobile populations in India, Aadhaar can be a major facilitator of portability of rights, whether to food security or education as we noted above; it can also be a vehicle for checking on ghost or duplicate members of SHGs.

While looking at the particular uses of Aadhaar, the overall issue is that of the main direction of development and the manner in which the poor participate in it. The poor at present secure some of their entitlements, such as food grain, through commodity distribution in the PDS system. Their economic interactions are largely of the informal variety. Own account workers in the urban informal sector, whether vegetable or other vendors, do not have rights to the spaces they occupy for their business and pay various amounts to street-level bureaucrats, including the police, slumlords and other such persons with local power.

In rural areas, to the extent that women work the land, they have no title to such land or even legal lease rights. The lack of legal ownership and lease rights keeps the women workers on informal agreements subject to exactions and also inhibits them from accessing credit to undertake investments with which they could increase their own productivity and incomes. Operation Barga in West Bengal in the late 1970s was an example of a major step in giving legal rights to 'informal' sharecroppers. It was a step which by all accounts empowered the sharecroppers and enabled them to undertake investment to increase productivity on the lands they now securely possessed. However, women and their independent rights as producers in agriculture were totally ignored.

How does one move forward from the present situation of widespread informality? As pointed out, specifically with reference to the Aadhaar debate (Maringanti, 2009: 39), there are those who would want to preserve the informality of the situation. There are others who argue that the way forward is towards formalisation of rights and responsibilities. Whether it is for the poor in general or for women in particular, formalisation of rights provides a platform for further economic and social advances. Here it should be pointed out that poor women are doubly disadvantaged, both as poor and as women, in informal transactions that are based on power relations.

Aadhaar opens up avenues for development in formal ways, as against the widespread informality currently prevailing. Power equations enter into formal transactions too. But when the poor and women have rights over the spaces they use, they can become stronger in these power equations.

9

Identity, Equality and Development

In the recent years, the civil society discussions across Asia Pacific regions have drawn attention to intra-country global inequalities as well as a rise in intra-country inequality in the emergent economies of China and India. The pattern of economic growth in China since the 1980s and in India since the 1990s had a strong impact on inequality in the countries, largely seen as a result of shift from agriculture to industry and from rural to urban areas. Discussing the intra-country inequality in the rising powers, a recent study noted that the Gini coefficient increased by 24 per cent in China and by 16 per cent in India during the decade 1990s to 2000s (Nathan and Sarkar, 2014: 280). Significantly disproving the Kuznets Curve, (i.e. income inequality would fall as societies modernised), Piketty (2014), in a massive analysis shows that inequality has exploded in the last 30 years almost everywhere, including the United States and the United Kingdom. Few dispute that women constitute a significant majority of the unequal populations throughout the world. UN Women's, women's organisations and individual feminist analysis have shown the structural causes of gender-based discrimination and exclusion resulting in high inequalities of women in social, political and economic spheres.

The gender division of labour and women's lack of an independent identity in distribution of income, property and productive inputs or technologies have major economic implications and result in gendered economic behaviour. The magnitude and intensity of unpaid work presupposes the forced labour of domestic caring by women in the reproductive sector. "In this context, domestic violence or its threat within the household can be seen first not as an extra-economic social problem but also a form of labour extraction" (Cagatay, 2003: 28).

Women's economic empowerment is increasingly being acknowledged as a prerequisite for sustainable development and inclusive growth. Such empowerment is about the rights of the poor and the excluded, and is part of an effort towards building equitable societies. In the past, there has been a general concern over improvements in conditions of health, education and the social well-being of women. It was, however, rarely recognised that such development is contingent on the realisation of women's economic empowerment and autonomy in the management and ownership of productive assets.

A recent study conducted by the International Center for Research on Women (ICRW) says that a woman may be considered economically empowered when she has the ability to succeed in her economic endeavours and the power of decision-making (Golla *et al.*, 2011). Such empowerment of women is critical to realise women's rights to achieve economic growth and social well-being.

The OECD–DAC Network on Gender Equality (GENDERNET) defines women's economic empowerment as women's "capacity to participate in, contribute to and benefit from growth processes in ways that recognise the value of their contributions, respect their dignity and make it possible to negotiate a fairer distribution of the benefits of growth" (OECD–DAC, 2011: 6). With an independent identity and voice, women's economic empowerment is both a process and an outcome; when women have a voice in the opportunities to obtain assets, property and inheritance, their overall social–economic standing improves, leading to dignity and freedom of different choices. Considering money as the measure of respect, women in rural Bangladesh, use the phrase *Garamtaka* (weighty money). It is money that has weight and gives identity to women within the household (Kelkar *et al.*, 2004: 24). For instance, in an anonymous collective discussion in rural Bangladesh, one woman said, "If you have no money, there is no value for your choice. You are sitting in a corner like a little thief with no identity and agency to your voice... if you have assets, everyone loves you" (Kelkar *et al.*, 2004: 24). Another woman, Gul Akhtar, who had recently acquired 1.5 decimals of agricultural land in her own name, said, "If we have sampotti (property and assets), our samman (dignity/identity/prestige) will be permanent. Samman is closely linked withsampotti" (Kelkar *et al.*, 2004: 34).

A paper for the Swedish International Development Agency (SIDA) defines women's economic empowerment as "the process which increases women's real power over economic decisions that influence their lives and priorities in society", which "can be achieved through equal access to and control over critical economic resources and opportunities, and the elimination of structural inequalities in the labour market including a better share of unpaid care work" (Tornqvist and Schmitz, 2009: 9). As noted elsewhere (Kelkar, 2007), rural women define their identity against patriarchal social norms. Women aspire to be economically independent and they do not want their daughters to experience societal pressure as they did in their own lives. Aspirations reflect people's hopes for the future and lead to the creation of new needs which bring in change in the economic and social base of existing capabilities. This, in turn, leads to a shift in the productive objective—from subsistence production to maximisation of income and saving-cum-accumulation to meet new needs. "I do not want my daughter to face this humiliation, so I want her to be educated and independent", says an indigenous Chenchu woman from Andhra Pradesh, India (Nathan and Kelkar, 2004).

In other parts of South Asia, there are rural women and semi-literate women who have stated their strategic need for dignity, which, according to them, comes from having complex knowledge of the outside world (as against a domesticated existence), access to markets and technology and, most importantly, with ownership and management of productive assets (Kelkar and Krishnaraj, 2013; Kelkar *et al.*, 2004). These voices of women suggest a change in the social norms of dependency and subjugation, and seek a culture of autonomy and empowerment with access to technology and control on productive assets.

The necessary elements of women's economic empowerment comprise a mix of identity, autonomy and dignity (associated with choice, mobility and freedom from violence); non-discrimination in work (associated with gender, parity of wages/rewards/remuneration, and rearrangement and counting of household work and care); and women's individual identity, unmediated right to ownership and management of productive assets (e.g. land, house, technology and finances). These, in turn, provide them with the capability to make decisions both within the home and outside in the labour market.

Economic empowerment for many scholars and women's rights' advocates, as seen in the preceding pages, has so far meant enhanced access to decision-making and increased control over productive assets. There is also a growing acceptance in development communities with regard to the association of empowerment with increased capabilities, and the independent identity which, in turn, expand freedom of choice and agency. Feminist analysts generally see the two essential conditions of empowerment: women's freedom from subjugation and their ability to achieve greater autonomy in management of their life and resources. The criteria for empowerment therefore require a transformative change in the existing relations of control and power over productive assets between women and men.

There are institutional requirements that support the development of capital, so to say, from above. Owners of property and investors require such institutional conditions in order to advance their businesses and thus develop production. But what about the institutional requirements for those who are not property owners, who are part of the capitalist economy; e.g., women who are defined as dependent on the male within the household economic structure.

In an illuminating analysis of the pre-industrial revolution development of Britain, Sretzer (2007) following Solar (1995) argues for the importance of the mid-17th century Elizabethean Poor Laws in conjunction with the 13th century establishment of alienability of land in encouraging "labor mobility and emancipation from a peasant mentality of over-attachment to land as the only form of security" (Sretzer, 2007: 73). The entitlements of the Poor Laws were portable so that wherever one moved, individuals had the certainty of being provided for. This enabled employers to adopt the most efficient production technologies, even if that meant the displacement of workers. Sretzer contrasts this with the situation in the European continent where there were greater fears and protests among those adversely affected.

Not only were migrating individuals protected by the universal entitlements, in England and Wales, women and men left behind in rural areas and other excluded groups could draw on parish funds for their subsistence support. This promoted migration or reduced its costs.

This ubiquitous system of social security depended on the prior existence of personal identities, established from before the 16th century. The combination of registered identity, combined with universalist and portable social protection, softened the transition from smallholder peasant to capitalist economy. Sretzer argues that it was this social protection system that enabled England, before the industrial revolution, to adopt the most efficient organic agricultural techniques and thus pull ahead of the Netherlands and coastal China in agricultural productivity.

In light of the above analysis, we can argue that the Aadhaar registration system is important in establishing the base for a national social minimum, with universal and portable entitlements. Given the ongoing turmoil over displacement and the frequent reluctance to sell land, creation of a universal and portable social protection system becomes necessary for carrying forward the process of creative destruction. It would reduce the over-reliance on the male as the provider or head of the household in terms of economic security. In general, it would reduce the opposition to change in the women's social-economic position, a process that is necessary for development.

The provision of universal and portable social security entitlements would have a number of developmental benefits. It would reduce the risks of migration and thus promote labour mobility. It would support women and other smallholders in undertaking higher productivity but riskier investments. It would provide an income base for the poorest households to invest in their children's education. Of course, for shifting out of traditional livelihoods, including shifting the surplus labour from agriculture, the creation of new jobs is necessary; but the existence of social protection would provide an assured minimum in the very likely gap between losing a livelihood and getting a job.

All of the above depends on the existence of an identity system. In multi-religious India, this identity system cannot be based on religious organisation, as was the case of the parish registration system in Elizabethan England. In current-day India, such an identity system will have to be non-religious and state-based.

Identity Construction and Changes in Gendered Structures

Our observations and individual and collective discussions during the fieldwork in the villages of Andhra Pradesh and Jharkhand indicate the strengthening of woman's individual identity, and an implicit move away from the traditional male-centred community identity structure.

The majority of Focus Group Discussion (FGD) participants (both women and men) reported some improvement in terms of the quality of housing, food and nutrition, health care, education and village infrastructure in the last 10-15 years. For both women and men, their identity as members of a household (or being a member of indigenous social group such as Munda and Oraon in case of Jharkhand) was clearly more important than their individual identity. However, women were keener to have an identity of their own; for men it was of less importance. The predominant source of household identity lies with the male head and other male members of the household, except in cases when a woman in the household holds an important public position (*mukhiya*, teacher, etc.). This identity gives the male head of the household a predominant role in the family decision-making process. For example, women always have to consult men on decisions related to expenses, savings or use of common resources. However, this is not the case with men. Men do not usually feel obliged to consult women on the use of the resources they earn or even the resources jointly earned or earned by the women. These roles are assumed and naturalised by both women and men. Men enjoy the status of the head of the household; what is important to note is that men did not resist the policy effort in according women an independent identity with the Aadhaar number.

The gender gap with rights to access and manage productive assets was seen to be decreasing, as men's income alone was no longer perceived as enough to run the household. However, the men's control in ownership of land, house, bank accounts and major household assets as well as of women's earnings is still significant.

There was, however, a trend towards change in women's gendered lower position. In Jharkhand, for example, certain traditional taboos such as prohibition on women's 'climbing the thatched roof' and the touching or using the plough still remain quite entrenched in all the villages visited. Interestingly, these taboos were no longer adhered to new situations, such as cemented rooftops and in cases of 'educated' (high school and above) girls and women. Women's employment in teaching and village-level development work such as Anganwadi workers was reported to have enhanced their position within the household, as income brought by them was seen by both women and men as vital for the well-being of the household members. Nevertheless, in both the fieldwork areas (Andhra Pradesh and Jharkhand) a great majority of women participants in FGDs reported about acts of male violence in their homes, especially when women try to take part in economic decision-making. Men perceived this as a threat to their conventional hegemony as the head of the household.

Gender Factor in Aadhaar Enrolment

Access to information on Aadhaar was reported to be relatively easy. The main source of information on Aadhaar seemed to be word of mouth starting from information at the *panchayat* level. Access to information on Aadhaar enrolment was not observed to have any gender difference. This could be explained by the fact that most of the women participants were engaged in economic activities outside the house (agriculture, other wage labour, MGNREGA in both the fieldwork areas in Andhra Pradesh and Jharkhand).

Level of actual delivery of Aadhaar card was observed to be mixed and without any gender difference. Many of the participants had not received the card even after almost a year of enrolment. Others with enrolment at the same date (in the same village and in the same household) or even much later had already received the card. These included both women and men. The most common problems and errors reported were wrong names on the card, enrolment done only on the basis of photo, erased finger-lines, and children not being enrolled in some villages. Even among women and men who had not enrolled/or not been able to enrol for the Aadhaar number, a keenness to be able to now enrol could be clearly seen. In no case was there reluctance on part of the residents to enrol due to the biometric nature of the identity. During the FGDs, most of the participants who had not yet enrolled demanded information on where to enrol at that stage.

There was a noticeable absence of women as Aadhaar officers in village-level enrolments in both Andhra Pradesh and Jharkhand. However, *panchayats* or villages with active women leaders played an important role in facilitating the Aadhaar enrolment process. All participants concurred that the presence of women enrolment officers would make women more at ease in the enrolment process.

No clear differences could be observed between the levels of women's and men's enrolments. This could be due to the indigenous culture of the Jharkhand region or due to the relatively high level of migration of men in Andhra Pradesh. The decision to enrol or not was usually a collective household decision and no preference to enrolment of male members of the household over women's enrolment was reported. This 'equal keenness' towards women's enrolment could have been influenced by: (i) relative ease of enrolment; and (ii) the fact that the Aadhaar card is widely expected to bring in some financial entitlements and benefits in the future. It was also interesting to note that even though both women and men said that women would have felt more comfortable around women enrolment officials, the fact that almost all enrolment officials were men did not act as a barrier for women to enrol in the programme.

In some villages, however, the enrolment of adults was given priority over enrolment of children; though in most villages children were also enrolled. One exception in this regard was the village of Jojahatu of Jharkhand.

The level of enrolment seemed to be higher in cases where the enrolment camps were set up at the village levels. When the enrolment centres were far, problems of distance, long queues, need to return the next day, etc., were reported. Some other problems reported with the enrolment camps were the camp duration being short and insufficient or the camp closing down on dates earlier than what had been initially announced.

Awareness about Aadhaar Identity

In general, a high level of awareness about the existence of the Aadhaar identity was observed between both women and men. On an average, around 90–95 per cent of the FGD participants in both areas of study (Andhra Pradesh and Jharkhand) reported being aware of the 'new' Aadhaar card.

Most of the participants were not aware of the potential uses and benefits of the Aadhaar identity beyond its use as a new ID card replacing other ID cards. Some of the reasons cited for Aadhaar enrolment were: "It was a new ID", "It will be useful in the future" and "Everyone was enrolling for the Aadhaar".

Most of the participants were not aware of the specific characteristics of Aadhaar, some of which were different from other existing IDs (portability, cardless nature of the Aadhaar numbers, voluntary enrolment, and so on). For example, it was reported that many migrant workers had come back to the village from as far as Delhi and Mumbai to register for Aadhaar enrolment in Jharkhand. On the one hand, this shows the keenness of people to enrol in Aadhaar, but, on the other hand, it shows that its portability and cardless nature is not completely understood as the migrant residents could have registered in the city of current residence.

Similarly, women (like men) were not aware of the implications of individual identity of women with the Aadhaar and the potential benefits that the Aadhaar identity could bring to women. This could be due to the fact that the Aadhaar awareness campaign does not include information on gender differentiated identity, benefits.

The perceived uses reported by women and men were largely similar. The most common possible uses cited for Aadhaar (by both women and men) were opening bank accounts, buying sim cards, followed by public works and services payments (mainly MGNREGA, and pension, especially in pilot villages).

Most of the women and men kept their card at home and hardly ever took it out with them. This can perhaps be explained by the early stages of the Aadhaar initiative and the fact that as yet very few public programmes had been linked to Aadhaar. Fear of losing the card was also cited as one of the reasons for not taking it out of the house unless needed for a specific purpose.

In East Godavari District, women perceived the Aadhaar card as unique and different from earlier identification documents as it gives them an individual identity; enables them to independently receive their entitlements; and can be used as a recognised individual identity proof anywhere in the country. Women in Ranga Reddy District said that the Aadhaar card could be used for multiple benefits, as a common card for accessing all government benefits. Women became a major clientele group through the SHGs. For example, they have been seen as focused groups for government programmes, like Deepam and IKP poverty reduction strategies. Aadhaar is seen as a value added product over the smart card, especially in terms of unique identification, which has centralised verification and a real time payment system.

Women unanimously stated that the Aadhaar card has increased their respect within the family. This is especially mentioned in East Godavari District, where women have been receiving the benefits from Aadhaar-linked services.

However, women said that the government should make further efforts towards educating the people about the benefits of Aadhaar. Women, across the two districts, said that Aadhaar is a better identity than other specific identity document. It makes them feel empowered. Women reported higher self-esteem by possessing an Aadhaar card. The researchers saw this when they saw the pride with which women showed their Aadhaar cards. Women further reiterated that they used the Aadhaar card for all government schemes and benefits and received them individually. They also used the cards for other purposes, such as buying a mobile phone sim card, opening a bank account, and so on. Importantly, women said that due to the Aadhaar identity and the related AEPS, men and officials too are more polite. Even shopkeepers and traders are polite while negotiating with women. Thus, women feel more confident in going outside the village to markets or visiting other towns; since if asked to identify themselves, they can show their Aadhaar cards. Women also said that with the Aadhaar-linked system of payment in various government schemes, correct targeting of women is possible and benefits would be received by them.

The existing patriarchal structures lead to a situation where the new Aadhaar identity cards are implicitly under the control of the male head of the household, which again limits its impact in the construction of a woman's individual identity. Reinforcing the individual and cardless character of the Aadhaar number should be a priority in explaining the potential benefits of Aadhaar-based identity.

Almost all the FGD participants (both women and men) had individual identities before Aadhaar. Most of them have had the voter ID card for some years. This made it difficult to observe the impact of the 'first' 'individual' identity on their (mainly women's) self-esteem, etc. Similarly, the voter ID card was accepted for purposes beyond just exercising political rights (voting); the most common being its use as an ID proof for banking, and to access public services and social protection programmes. This makes it difficult to gauge the added value of the new Aadhaar cards as the comparison is not so much between 'no individual ID' and an 'individual ID', but between 'the old' (voter card) and the 'new' (Aadhaar) individual ID. However, this perception of 'value added' could perhaps be observed better once Aadhaar is actually linked to multiple public programmes.

10

Conclusions

Improving Women's Capabilities with Identity and Technology

Throughout the fieldwork, we noted that women wanted to improve their lives in new ways. They have begun to view the marketplace, and not the household, as the driver of modern technological society. They wanted to improve their working lives associated with independent identities and new technologies, and wanted to improve their abilities and talents to participate in technological change in the rural society. Our analysis further indicates that the architects of Aadhaar technology had limited orientation to create an identity technology that would be responsive to women's needs. The gender outcome of Aadhaar in terms of social gains of increased autonomy and agency of women has been an unintentional consequence of a technological design that accords women new configurations with an independent identity.

There are two problems with regard to gender concerns in Aadhaar's socio-technical system. First, there is the problem of identifying inequalities and the much needed attention for women's unmediated identity in the process of Aadhaar implementation. The second problem is that the socio-technical system of Aadhaar is instituted without sharply delineated criteria of bringing positive change in women's position or in altering gender relations.

In most of the study areas, women expressed great keenness to possess Aadhaar cards, particularly those who had not yet received their Aadhaar cards; this is despite the fact that many components of Aadhaar benefits were not always completely known. In one of the research sites in the Jharkhand countryside, women categorically stated that in this early stage of the Aadhaar process, it was not possible to predict the chains of benefits from the Aadhaar identity.

In this regard, we would like to remind ourselves that the telephone was designed as a business device to send out short messages. Women used it as a means of breaking out of their domestic isolation and connecting themselves into a social group that could provide support in crisis and in their daily life.

Some actions that would bring about a change in women's lives with Aadhaar technology would be: to understand the full benefits of Aadhaar, the government, through subdistrict and district centres, needs to create more awareness about the various public services/ schemes that can be accessed with the Aadhaar identity. This can be addressed through capacity development meetings/workshops at the village level in *gram sabhas* and through electronic and print media, and discussions in rural women's groups, such as SHGs to explain the benefits of Aadhaar to women and men who lag behind in literacy, freedom of mobility and in voicing their strategic interests.

It is also important to create more awareness about those aspects of Aadhaar such as the individual, biometric and cardless nature; the non-specific purpose identity that make it unique and set it apart from previous identifications held by women, men and households. The awareness of its exact nature should be combined with a greater understanding of how Aadhaar can act as an instrument for the empowerment of women.

The positive example of Andhra Pradesh (with an extremely active self-help group [SHGs] network) should be used to promote greater involvement of SHGs and other women's organisations in creating a greater understanding of Aadhaar and in the process of Aadhaar enrolment, and in linking Aadhaar to diverse services. An active involvement of women's organisations in these processes combined with an appropriate system of feedback would also help identify further suggestions to maximise Aadhaar's potential for social inclusion.

Even as, conceptually, Aadhaar holds a huge potential for increased social inclusion, greater attention needs to be paid to it's on the ground implementation to ensure that this objective is not lost sight of due to the huge scale of the programme. In this sense, some basic gender/social inclusion sensitisation training could be imparted to the implementing officers to ensure that the enrolment process itself is inclusive and does not leave out members of the most marginalised communities due to the greater difficulty in registering them and the inherent biases of the enrolment officers. Ensuring the presence of women officers in the enrolment teams would be another step in this direction.

One of the most important social inclusion benefits of Aadhaar is its role in facilitating greater inclusion of the most marginalised sections of the population in the mainstream financial system. To this end, agreements have been entered into with different financial service providers, which, if implemented as planned, could turn out to be a game changer for both the country's financial system as well for the sections of the population currently outside the formal financial system. However, there have been reports of problems in the ground implementation of these facilities. This merits greater attention to ensure that the financial inclusion objective of Aadhaar is effectively achieved.

Enrolment centres need to be opened in every *panchayat* for easy access to enrolment. There should be special centres for women, especially for elderly and pregnant, and those with small children. There is a need to set up women's bank branches at the subdistrict level which will facilitate the financial inclusion of rural women.

During the fieldwork in Andhra Pradesh, we observed that some women were employed in the risky situations of managing a considerable amount of cash for the Aadhaar-enabled Payment System (AEPS) disbursal at the village level. However, at the higher level of Aadhaar implementation in subdistrict and district levels, there was a noticeable absence of women. This needs policy attention to include more women in adequate numbers in the management of AEPS at the subdistrict and district levels. Further, these women need to be insured for any physical injury while conducting their assigned duties.

The rural institution of SHGs requires special attention with regard to the further development of their capabilities. An important outcome of the SHG network and its social mobilisation will be to enable women to play a substantial role in reduction of household poverty and inequality, and in creating a socio-technical space for women's independent identity and agency. With some gender responsive production training, these groups of women would be able to negotiate to bring their knowledge, needs, preferences, views and experiences of technology and its social, gender context to identity needed in production and marketing.

Lastly, as we saw earlier, even as greater social inclusion (including inclusion of women) is a key objective of the Aadhaar initiative, the programme does not explicitly aim at women's greater empowerment. However, as is clear from this study, the programme can play an important role towards greater autonomy, identity and empowerment of women; especially rural women and women belonging to the socially and economically marginalised sections. Recognising this potential, linkages could be made between Aadhaar and the different public programmes aimed at women's empowerment, resulting in yet another kind of convergence that would enrich a multipronged strategy towards shifts in the gendered power structures in the country.

A social, gender transformative agenda with Aadhaar identity and AEPS requires re-scripting women's role in the economic development, and doing away with lingering features and embedded ideas about women's household-based marginal identity in the process of development. Capability development is not just a technical skill; it is a combination of knowledge, skills, identity for effective ownership or possession of productive assets that can be translated into transforming social (and individual) attitudes and actions. Women's strategic interest for autonomous/empowered functioning within the home and outside are to be seen as part of technology design, and not merely a policy sympathy for women's economic and social rights. This further means addressing the issue of change in the hierarchy and power base of gender relations and the consequent improvement in women's autonomy and agency. Notwithstanding the initial efforts in creation of the UID, the mere existence of a socio-technical space for individual identity of women carries the seed of new gender relations.

References

Abraham, Neenu (2012). "Technology Use to Make PDS Purchase a Breeze", *The Economic Times*, 30 October.

Acemoglu, Daron and James Robinson (2013). *Why Nations Fail: The Origins of Power, Prosperity and Poverty.* London: Profile Books.

Akerlof, G.A. and R. Kranton (2010). *Identity Economics: How Our Identities Shape Our Work, Wages and Well-Being.* Princeton: Princeton University Press.

Aneka (2011). *Transgender People and Unique Identification Number.* Bangalore.

Basu, Kaushik (2000). *Prelude to Political Economy: A Study of the Social and Political Foundations of Economics.* New Delhi: Oxford University Press.

Bharat, Bhatti and Madhulika Khanna (2012). "Neither Effective nor Equitable", *The Hindu.* 4 December.

Bourdieu, P. (2001). *Masculine Domination* (Translated by Richard Nice). Stanford, CA: Stanford University Press.

Cagatay, N. (2003). "Engendering Macro-Economics", in M. Gutierrez (ed.), *Macro-Economics: Making Gender Matter, Concept, Policies and Institutional Changes in Developing Countries.* London and New York: Zed Books. pp.22-41.

Centre for Economic and Social Studies (2012). *Approach to the 12th Five Year Plan of Andhra Pradesh.* Hyderabad.

Chaudhuri, A.R. and E. Somanathan (2011). "Impact of Biometric Identification-Based Transfer", *Economic and Political Weekly* 46(21) : 77–80.

Dreze, Jean and Amartya Sen (2013). *An Uncertain Glory: India and its Contradictions.* New Delhi: Allen Lane, The Penguin Press.

Duflo, E. (2012). "Women's Economic Empowerment and Economic Development", *NBER Working Paper* 17702. Cambridge, M.A.: National Bureau of Economic Research.

EGovernment Reach (2013). "Aadhaar Card Mandatory for Government School Students in Jharkhand", 18 April. *http://egovreach.in/social/content/Aadhaar-card-mandatory-govt-school-students-jharkhand* (last accessed on 13 August 2013).

Folbre, Nancy (1994). *Who Pays for the Kids? Gender and the Structures of Constraints.* London and New York: Routledge.

Food and Civil Supplies Department, GoAP and Unique Identification Authority of India (UIDAI): (n.d.). *Public Distribution System: The Aadhaar Way.*

Galab, S. and N. Chandrasekhar (2003). "Women and Self Help Groups: Poverty Alleviation and Empowerment", in C.H. Hanumantha Rao and S. Mahendra Dev (eds.), *Andhra Pradesh Development: Economic Reforms and Challenges Ahead.* Hyderabad: Centre for Economic and Social Studies,

Gelb, Alan, and Julia Clark (2012). "Identification for Development: The Biometrics Revolution", *Working Paper* 315. Centre for Global Development. *www.cgdev.org* (last accessed on 14-11-12).

———. (2013). "Identification for Development: The Bio-metrics Revolution", *Working Paper* 315. Centre for Global Development.

Ghoshal, Devjyot (2012). "As Aadhaar Debuts in Jharkhand, Doubts Arise", *Business Standard*, 4 April.

GoAP and CESS (2007). *Human Development Report 2007: Andhra Pradesh*. Hyderabad: Government of Andhra Pradesh and Centre for Economic and Social Studies.

Golla, A., A. Malhotra, P. Nanda and R. Mehra (2011). *Understanding and Measuring Women's Economic Empowerment; Definition, Framework, Indicators*. Washington DC: International Centre for Research on Women.

Hamza, Amir Syed and Nitesh Narain (2013). *Aadhar Enabled Direct Benefit Transfer in East Godavari*. Microsave

Hanlon, Joseph, Armando Barrientos and David Hulme (2010). *Just Give Money to the Poor: The Development Revolution from the Global South*. Sterling: Kumarian Press.

International Monetary Fund (IMF) (2013). *Regional Economic Outlook: Asia and the Pacific*. Washington, DC: International Monetary Fund.

Johnson, Doug (2008/11). *Case Study on the Use of Smartcard to Deliver Government Benefits in Andhra Pradesh*, India, *http://dx.doi.org/10.2.21/ssrn_1886014* (last accessed on 12 May 2013).

Kainth, Gursharan Singh (2011). *Aadhar India: Brand for Billion*. Saabrucken, LAP Lambert: Academic Publication.

Kelkar, G. (2007). *The Feminization of Agriculture in Asia: Implications for Women's Agency and Productivity*. Taipei, Taiwan: Food and Fertilizer Technology Centre.

———. (2013). "The Fog of Entitlement: Women and Land in India", Paper Presented at the *World Bank Conference on Land and Poverty.* April 8-11.

Kelkar, Govind and Dev Nathan (2002). "Gender Relations and Technological Change in Asia", *Current Sociology* 50(3): 427–41.

Kelkar, G. and M. Krishnaraj (eds.) (2013). *Women, Land and Power in Asia*. Routledge, India.

Kelkar, G., D. Nathan and R. Jahan (2004). "Redefining Women's 'Samman': Micro-Credit and Gender Relations in Rural Bangladesh", *Economic and Political Weekly* 30(32): 3627-40.

Levy, Santiago (2008). *Good Intentions, Bad Outcomes: Social Policy, Informality and Economic Growth in Mexico.* Washington, DC: Brookings Institution Press.

Lindert, Peter (2004).*Growing Public: Social Spending and Economic Growth since the Eighteenth Century*, Cambridge: Cambridge University Press.

Maringanti, Anand (2009). "Sovereign States and the Mobile Subjects", *Economic and Political Weekly* 44(46): 35-40.

Mehdudia, Sujay (2012). "Nearly a Fourth of all LPG Connections are Fake", *The Hindu*, 31 October.

Narayan, Santosh (2013). "Nilekani Stresses on e-Aadhaar Printing Facility", *The Pioneer*, 10 April.

Nathan, Dev and Alakh N. Sharma (2012). "Migration, Cash Transfers and Social Security", *Yojana*. New Delhi: Planning Commission of India.

Nathan, D. and G. Kelkar (2004). "Women's Empowerment in the Market Place and Household: Good Practice", *Study on Chinchu People.* New Delhi: UNIFEM.

Nathan, D. and S. Sarkar (2014). "Global Inequality, Rising Power and Labour Standards", *Oxford Development Studies* 42(2): 278-95, June.

National Institute of Public Finance and Policy (NIPFP) (2012). *A Cost-Benefit Analysis of Aadhaar.* NIPFP-Macro Finance Group. *http://macrofinance.nipfp.org.in* (last accessed on 10 June 2013).

Nayar, Pramod K. (2012). "I Sing the Body Biometric: Surveillance and Biological Citizenship", *Economic and Political Weekly* 47(32): 17–22.

NCAER (National Council of Applied Economic Research) (2005). *Comprehensive Study to Assess the Genuine Demand and Development of SKO (Special Kerosene Oil).* Technical Report M/05/079. http://www.ncaer.org/downloads/Annual Reports/Annual Reports_2005.pdf. Accessed on 28th March, 2014.

North, Douglass (2005). *Understanding the Process of Economic Change.* Princeton and Oxford: Princeton University Press.

OECD-DAC Network on Gender Equality (2011). "Women's Economic Empowerment", *Issues Paper.* April.

Piketty, Thomas (2014). *Capital in the 21st Century.* Cambridge: Harvard University Press.

Planning Commission (2010). "From Exclusion to Inclusion with Micropayments", *Working Paper.* UIDAI, Planning Commission, Government of India. *http://uidai.gov.in/UID_PDF/Front_Page_Articles/Strategy/Exclusion_to_Inclusion_with_Micropayments.pdf* (last accessed on 13 August 2013).

___(2012). *Aadhaar Enabled Service Delivery.* UIDAI, Planning Commission, Government of India. *http://uidai.gov.in/images/authDoc/whitepaper_aadhaarenabledservice_delivery.pdf* (last accessed on 13 August 2013).

Ramanathan, Usha (2010). "A Unique Identity Bill", *Economic and Political Weekly* 45(30): 10–14.

Rao, Ursula (2013). "Biometric Marginality, UID and the Shaping of Homeless Identities in the City", *Economic and Political Weekly* 48(13): 71–77.

Rawat, V.S. (2012). "Google Earth Scanner for UP Job Scheme", *Business Standard,* 14 November.

Reddy, D. Narismha and Dev Nathan (2012). *Alternative Policy Instrument for Poverty Reduction: A Comparative Study of Andhra Pradesh and Bihar.* New Delhi: Institute of Human Development.

Revathi, E. (1998). *Women, Work and Technology in Indian Agriculture: A Study in Andhra Pradesh.* Rohtak: Spellbound Publication.

———. (2010). "Women and Land". Unpublished paper

———. (2012). *Land Access to Women and Women Empowerment under Different Situations in Andhra Pradesh.* Report submitted to ICSSR under fellowship programme.

Rodgers, G., Amrita Datta, Janine Rodgers, Sunil K. Mishra and Alakh N. Sharma (2012). *The Challenge of Inclusive Development in Rural Bihar.* IHD and Manak Publications Pvt. Ltd.

Schmidt, E. and J. Cohen (2013). *The New Digital Age: Reshaping the Future of People.* London: John Murray.

Scott, James C. (1998). *Seeing Like a State.* New Haven: Yale University Press.

Sen, Amartya.(2009). 'The Fog of Identity', *Politics, Philosophy and Economics* 8: 285–88.

SEWA Bharat (2012). *An Experimental Cash Transfer Study in Delhi.* GNCTD-UNDP, Government of Delhi.

SEWA and UNICEF (2012). *Unconditional Cash Transfers: Findings from Two Pilot Studies*. Conference Report. May 30-31. New Delhi.

Sharma, R.S. (2010). "Identity and the UIDAI: A Response", *Economic and Political Weekly* 45(35): 101–03.

Shukla, Ravi (2010). "Reimagining Citizenship: Debating India's Unique Identification Scheme", *Economic and Political Weekly* 45(2): 31–36.

Solar, P.M. (1995). "Poor Relief and English Economic Development Before the Industrial Revolution", *Economic History Review* 48(1): 1–22.

Srivastava, R.R. (2013). "Come October, Aadhaar Must for Gas Connections", *The Pioneer.* Hazaribagh. 13 June.

Sretzer, Simon (2007). "The Right of Registration: Development, Identity Registration, and Social Development : A Historical Perspective", *World Development* 35(2): 67–86

Task Force (2011). *Interim Report of the Task Force in Direct Transfer of Subsidies on Kerosene, LPG and Fertilizer*. Unpublished.

The Hindu (2012). "No Need for Hype But Certainly a Hope", *The Hindu,* 11 December

———. (2013). "Cash Transfers Can Help Make India Less Unequal, But are Not a Magic Bullet", 10 January

The Pioneer (2013a). "Come September, Aadhaar Card Mandatory for Salary and Pension", *The Pioneer,* 31 May.

———. (2013b). "JSY Beneficiaries' Aadhaar Cards to be Seeded with Bank Accounts", *The Pioneer,* 14 June.

———. (2013c). "Aadhaar Becomes POI for Government Services in Jharkhand", *The Pioneer* Ranchi edition, 14 May.

The Telegraph (2013). "Aadhaar Numbers for State by Year-End", *The Telegraph,* 10 April.

Times of India (2012). "2nd Phase Aadhaar Enrolment in April 3rd Week", *Times of India,* 11 April.

Tornqvist, A. and C. Schmitz (2009). "Women's Economic Empowerment: Steps for SIDA's Engagement", *Working Paper*. SIDA.

Unique Identification Authority of India (2014). Web Portal: *http://uidai.gov.in/*. Government of India. 18 June.

Zelazny, Frances (2012). "The Evolution of India's UID Program: Lessons Learned and Implications for Other Developing Countries"", *CGD Policy Paper* 008, August. *www.cgdev.org* (last accessed on 30 April 2013).

About HBF

The Heinrich Böll Stiftung/Foundation (HBF) is the Green Political foundation from Germany, affiliated to the "Greens/Alliance'90", political party represented in the Germany's federal parliament.

Headquartered in Berlin and with 30 international offices today, HBS conducts and supports civic educational activities and projects worldwide.

HBF understands itself as a green think-tank and international policy network, working with governmental and non-governmental actors and focusing on gender equity, sustainable development, and democracy and human rights.

With a presence in New Delhi since 2002, the HBF India office coordinates the interaction with stakeholders and partners in the country. Its programme focus areas include climate and resource policy, socio-economic policy from a gender perspective, the dynamics of democracy, and India's role in the new global order.